The Personality of Shakespeare

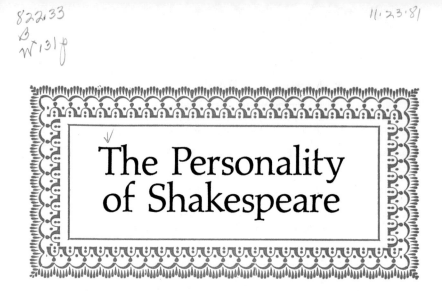

The Personality
of Shakespeare

Edward Wagenknecht

University of Oklahoma Press
Norman

RECENT BOOKS BY EDWARD WAGENKNECHT

Nathaniel Hawthorne, Man and Writer (New York, 1961)
Mark Twain: The Man and His Work (Norman, 1961, 1967)
Washington Irving: Moderation Displayed (New York, 1962)
The Movies in the Age of Innocence (Norman, 1962)
Edgar Allan Poe: The Man Behind the Legend (New York, 1963)
Chicago (Norman, 1964)
Seven Daughters of the Theater (Norman, 1964)
Harriet Beecher Stowe: The Known and the Unknown (New York, 1965)
Dickens and the Scandalmongers: Essays in Criticism (Norman, 1965)
The Man Charles Dickens: A Victorian Portrait (Norman, 1966)
Henry Wadsworth Longfellow: Portrait of an American Humanist (New York, 1966)
Merely Players (Norman, 1966)
John Greenleaf Whittier, A Portrait in Paradox (New York, 1967)
The Personality of Chaucer (Norman, 1968)
As Far as Yesterday: Memories and Reflections (Norman, 1968)
The Supernaturalism of New England, by John Greenleaf Whittier, edited by E. W. (Norman, 1969)
William Dean Howells: The Friendly Eye (New York, 1969)
Marilyn Monroe: A Composite View, edited by E. W. (Philadelphia, 1969)
The Personality of Milton (Norman, 1970)
James Russell Lowell: Portrait of a Many-Sided Man (New York, 1971)
Ambassadors for Christ: Seven American Preachers (New York, 1972)

Library of Congress Cataloging in Publication Data
Wagenknecht, Edward Charles, 1900–
    The personality of Shakespeare.
    Includes bibliographical references.
    1. Shakespeare, William, 1564–1616—Biography. 2. Shakespeare, William, 1564–1616—Criticism and interpretation. I. Title.
PR2909.W3   822.3'3   72–868
ISBN 0-8061-1028-7

*In memory of the Department of English at
The University of Chicago in the early 1920's,
where I learned what I know of scholarship,
and especially of my friend,
Professor Albert Harris Tolman,
who taught me how to read Shakespeare*

PREFACE

Shakespeare's famous "objectivity" might seem to make him a less rewarding subject for character study than either Chaucer or Milton, whom I have already considered in the first two volumes of the trilogy which I here complete. Yet the adjective "Shakespearean" is not quite without meaning, nor was Ellen Terry quite mad when she called the dramatist the only man she had ever really loved. Bernard Shaw exaggerated grossly when he declared that with the plays and the sonnets in our hands we know more about Shakespeare than we do about Dickens or Thackeray. But so did Leon Howard when he found Shakespeare's work "characterless," not reflecting an individual personality, and he went far beyond Shaw in his recklessness when he drew from this supposition the wholly unwarranted conclusion that "the more poet, the less character; I cannot find that Shakespeare had any at all." The study of human personality inevitably involves judgment, evaluation, interpretation, and all these are partial and fallible. In the last analysis, the difference between studying Shakespeare's character and not Chaucer's or Milton's merely but even that of a modern writer for whom we have letters, journals, and the

reminiscences of friends, is more a difference in degree than in kind.

My main reliance, as the reader will observe, is the Shakespearean text itself, but this has necessarily been viewed in the light of everything I know about Shakespearean scholarship and criticism, old and new. The ultimate sources of many of my ideas are lost beyond recall, and I have used my footnotes, such as they are, to document my quotations and to discuss marginal matters.

In spite of everything that has been said about Shakespeare's objectivity, a great many writers have preceded me in trying to describe his personality, and I have supplemented my own findings by reprinting two earlier essays in the appendix. Gamaliel Bradford almost worshiped Shakespeare ("Ah! how that Shakespeare says everything!" he once wrote me), and in one of his best sonnets he called the Elizabethan drama "land of my first love, garden of my heart!" Yet he himself never turned out a fully developed psychograph of the dramatist. The piece here reprinted was intended for high-school students, being one of seven such studies which Bradford had practically completed at the time of his death; in *Portraits and Personalities* they were published by an editor, Mabel A. Bessey, who added to them five other character portraits which she chose from his previous volumes. Professor Manly's lecture—the work of a writer universally regarded as one of the great scholars of his time—is older, having been written for the University of Texas celebration of the tercentenary of Shakespeare's death.

The Bard himself speaks in these pages from *The Complete Plays and Poems of William Shakespeare*, New Cambridge Edition, edited by William Allan Neilson and Charles Jarvis Hill (Houghton Mifflin Company, 1942), by permission of, and arrangement with, the publishers.

West Newton, Mass.   E. W.
September 5, 1972

CONTENTS

The Personality of Shakespeare

The following abbreviations are employed in the footnotes:

A   Edward Arnold
CUP   Cambridge University Press
D   Doubleday and Company (under all firm names em-
            ployed)
Du   E. P. Dutton and Company
HB   Harcourt, Brace and Company (under all firm names
            employed)
HM   Houghton Mifflin Company
HUP   Harvard University Press
M   The Macmillan Company
OUP   Oxford University Press
PMLA   *Publications of the Modern Language Association*
UCP   The University of Chicago Press
VP   The Viking Press
YUP   Yale University Press

I

SOME GUIDELINES

A poet, says John Keats, "is the most unpoetical of anything in existence, because he has no identity; he is continually in for and filling some other body." But Walt Whitman wrote in the margin: "The great poet absorbs the identity of others, and the experience of others, and they are definite in him or from him; but he perceives them all through the powerful press of himself." Here is a direct conflict of first principles. The dramatic imagination goes forth out of itself and achieves its expression through animating or identifying itself with other personalities, remembered or created or recreated. So did Shakespeare, and so did Keats, at least during the period when he aspired toward a Shakespearean universality. Whitman—and the Whitman type of creative artist—on the other hand, instead of projecting himself into the world, creates by dramatizing his own personality. He himself said of *Leaves of Grass* that it represented the attempt

of a naive, masculine, affectionate, contemplative, sensual, imperious person to cast into literature not only his own grit and arrogance, but his own flesh and form, undraped, regardless of

3

models, regardless of modesty or law; and ignorant, as at first it appears, of . . . all outside of the fiercely loved land of his birth.

This does not mean that, as he conceived it, *Leaves of Grass* had only a personal significance (had this been the case, he would have done better to keep it to himself), for he was trying

to put a *Person*, a human being (myself, in the latter half of the nineteenth century, in America), freely, fully and truly on record. I could not find any similar personal record in current literature that satisfied me.

What he is saying essentially is that though he concentrates upon himself, he is interested in himself for his representative character. In himself he intends to show humanity; through himself he hopes to reveal the life of his time. Nevertheless, all this is to be filtered through his own individuality. "I, Walt Whitman" remains firmly fixed in the center of the stage, and whatever the reader sees must be viewed through his eyes. And Whitman's way was, with variations, also the way of Byron, Mark Twain, Ernest Hemingway, and many more; in a vastly larger, more intellectual, less narrowly personal way, it was even that of Milton.

I do not intend to debate the relative merits of these two different types of writer, though I think most of us will find it difficult not to feel that the Shakespearean type is vaster and wider. There can be no doubt that he achieves a greater fecundity. Willa Cather once declared that all the materials of her fictions had been gathered before she was fifteen; since then she had only been recollecting and reassembling. You would not expect such a writer to be prolific, or if she was, you would expect her to repeat herself considerably. You would also look for long waits between her books, for she would have but one well to draw from, and she would need to spend much of her time waiting for the well to fill up. Ernest Hemingway was not really a prolific writer either, and as he grew older, he spent more and more time imitating himself. And though Mark Twain may seem an exception to the rule, the exception is more apparent than real, for though he wrote a great

deal, the product was very uneven. Nearly all his best work derives from his memories of Hannibal, and he often keeps us there even when he seems to be writing about the Middle Ages.

It has always been recognized that special care must be taken in seeking expressions of personality in the work of writers of fiction. The essayist addresses his readers *in propria persona,* and though he may not in all cases expect to be taken literally, at least it is not necessary to be forever discriminating between that which is meaningful to the writer himself and that which has validity only for the character who utters it. It is true, of course, that when we find an interest reappearing in, say, play after play or an opinion expressed, perhaps repeatedly, in contexts where it does not seem called for by the situation presented, we have a right to suppose that this relates to a matter in which the writer himself felt considerable interest, but the application of this rule is not simple, and it is difficult to make it cover all contingencies. A dramatist may be (and generally is) sympathetic toward some characters and antipathetic toward others; he may even have a "chorus character" which he employs as a surrogate for himself. And a statement which seems completely at home in a dramatic context may still have a personal meaning for the dramatist if only the reader could find it out.

In *Twelfth Night* (II, 4) Viola, disguised as Cesario but secretly in love with her master, the Duke Orsino, is quizzed by him as follows:

DUKE.   Thou dost speak masterly.
        My life upon't, young though thou art, thine eye
        Hath stay'd upon some favour that it loves.
        Hath it not, boy?
VIOLA.   A little, by your favour.
DUKE.   What kind of woman is't?
VIOLA.   Of your complexion.
DUKE.   She is not worth thee, then. What years, i'faith?
VIOLA.   About your years, my lord.
DUKE.   Too old, by heaven. Let still the woman take

5

An elder than herself; so wears she to him,
So sways she level in her husband's heart.
For, boy, however we do praise ourselves,
Our fancies are more giddy and unfirm,
More longing, wavering, sooner lost and worn,
Than women's are.

VIOLA.   I think it well, my lord.

DUKE.   Then let thy love be younger than thyself,
Or thy affection cannot hold the bent.
For women are as roses, whose fair flower
Being once display'd, doth fall that very hour.

VIOLA.   And so they are; alas, that they are so!
To die, even when they to perfection grow!

Shakespeare, aged eighteen, married Anne Hathaway, twenty-six. Was he thinking of his own marriage when he wrote these lines, and if so are we to suppose that the marriage was unhappy?

On first consideration, we might seem to have a perfect case here. Malone, Coleridge, Richard Grant White, and Sir Sidney Lee all thought so. There is nothing, we say, in the dramatic situation presented in this scene which should make it necessary to debate any marriage problems.

Actually, however, this is weak reasoning. Whether Shakespeare's marriage was happy or unhappy, and whether or not he attributed its hypothetical unhappiness to the greater age of his wife, it is not reasonable to believe that this personally reserved and highly objective writer would drag the discussion of such a matter into one of his comedies. We may grant that, since he presumably had some recollections of his own experiences, he could hardly have written these lines without remembering that he and Anne must have fallen under Orsino's condemnation. But is this really important? With so wide-ranging a dramatist as Shakespeare must not something like it have happened many times, in many different connections? Was he making a personal confession and doing public penance whenever he touched upon anything he had ever experienced in any of his plays? The people

6

who first saw *Twelfth Night* presumably neither knew nor cared anything about the circumstances of Shakespeare's marriage; if he was writing about them here, then he was the "poet talking to himself" about which we have heard so much during recent years. Orsino's view, like most of the moralizing in Shakespeare, is thoroughly conventional, and ninety-nine out of a hundred people would agree with it. Moreover, it is by no means certain that it is unmotivated by the dramatic situation. "Cesario" is a woman, not a man, and she loves a man, not a woman, who is considerably older than she is. If the Duke understood the true situation, he would quite approve of her love, as before the end of the play he does; thus the irony of the situation is deepened.[1]

Differentiation between the dramatist and his characters is, however, by no means the only problem that arises in connection with the study of Shakespeare's personality. A play—or a story—is essentially neither a confession nor a sermon, and every writer of fiction knows how the characters may insist upon going their own way, regardless of the plans their creator has made for them. To be true to itself, his creation must sometimes break away from his personal tastes and convictions, and he may find himself writing almost exclusively out of consideration for the needs of the story or the exigencies of the situation into which his characters have been thrust. A successful work of art, in other words, must be true to itself even before it is true to its creator.

Noncreators generally ignore this element altogether, but it is especially important for a writer like Shakespeare, who borrowed many of his plots, ready-made, from traditional material whose mores had already become old-fashioned in his time and are well-nigh incomprehensible in ours. To be sure, he often alters the

---

[1] Albert H. Tolman discusses this and three other passages in "Shakespeare's Supposed References to his Marriage," *Falstaff and Other Shakespearean Topics* (M, 1925). The others seem to me adequately explained in terms of generalities, though Manly supports the autobiographical interpretation of *The Winter's Tale* (III, 3:59–65), as Tolman notes and as readers of my appendix will discover for themselves. I grant that nothing in *The Tempest* should have seemed to make Prospero's charge to Ferdinand in Act IV, Scene 1 necessary, but surely it is more natural to interpret this passage as an aging dramatist's sermon to youth rather than a personal confession.

borrowed material, and such alterations may very well illuminate his own attitude. But there were a great many things, like Hamlet's feigned madness, which he could not change or omit even if the play he turned out could make no really vital use of them. Such things had to be accepted, like the fairy tale convention that it is the third brother who succeeds in the quest or the folklore situation of the suitor who is rewarded with the hand of the princess if he guesses the answer to the riddle but loses his life if he does not.[2] Look at the beginning of *The Comedy of Errors*, where an insane Ephesian law condemns to death any Syracusan who should come to Ephesus. Aegeon falls under this condemnation, and the Duke Solinus, incredibly presented as a wise and humane man, reluctantly condemns him. Of course he is delivered at the end of the play, for in a really satisfying work of fiction you can always have your cake and eat it too. In *A Midsummer Night's Dream* the situation is, if possible, even worse, for unless Hermia shall wed the man her father chooses for her, she must either die or enter a nunnery. And here, too, Duke Theseus, like Solinus, finally cavalierly sets aside the law, though he has previously regarded himself as bound by it. In a story set in the remote past, the Elizabethan audience could apparently accept the inherited irrational situation, though it would very likely have rebelled had the sentence been carried out. From all this are we to draw the conclusion that Shakespeare was so insensitive as not to perceive the inhumanity of such a law, or of that monstrous *pater familias* of the *Dream*, compared to whom even Capulet might be called permissive?[3] Nothing, of course, could be more absurd. We are

---

[2] Shakespeare—or somebody—used this situation in *Pericles*, and in *All's Well That Ends Well* Helena (amazingly) is to die if she fails to cure the King. But in *The Merchant of Venice* the old folklore situation is softened. The defeated suitors do not die but must merely vow to remain unwed, and since the test has been so set up that only the man of insight can make the right choice, it should be comparatively easy for the audience to accept this. Centuries later we are still using the traditional situation in Puccini's *Turandot*, but now it is heavily psychologized, the Princess being a warped or psychopathic character who is healed and saved through a lover's devotion.

[3] In *The Merry Wives of Windsor* Mrs. Page wishes to marry her daughter to that fool Slender, but her husband prefers the well-heeled, tempery Dr. Caius, rather than wed whom the girl would prefer to be buried alive or boiled to death

dealing not with life but with a play, and the dramatist simply accepts the inherited situation and builds upon it for his convenience.

The Elizabethan drama had conventions of its own also, and we can ignore them only at our peril. So accomplished a Shakespearean as Richard Grant White once suggested that in order to make it seem credible that neither her father nor her lover should recognize Rosalind when they meet her in Arden, her figure should be padded, her face stained with umber, and her hair tied up in knots! Who would bother to go to the theater to see such a Rosalind he did not stop to inquire, and the ignorance of the Elizabethan theater which such a suggestion shows is appalling. For the Elizabethan drama is full of girls who disguise themselves as boys, and none of them are recognized until it suits the needs of the drama that they should be. This is purely a matter of dramatic convention (the element of "given"), and it must be accepted as such. Bassanio and Gratiano do not recognize their wives when they appear in the courtroom at Venice. Nor does the convention apply only to girls. Lear does not penetrate the disguise of Kent. Edmund does not recognize Edgar when he comes out to fight with him and slay him. In *The Winter's Tale* Florizel does not recognize his own father when the latter spies upon his love affair with Perdita, and none of the Duke's associates know who he is when he moves among them incognito in *Measure for Measure*.

In plays like *Measure for Measure*, moreover, this is the least of the conventional elements by which we are confronted. Realistically (that is, irrelevantly) considered, all the complicated intrigue with which this play ends is so much nonsense. If the Duke wished

---

with turnips. Are we supposed to conclude that Shakespeare believed such conduct to lie within the range of decent parents or even that it could conceivably be postulated of the characters he has created? As soon as both parents have been outwitted, and their daughter comfortably married to young Fenton, whom she loves, everybody accepts the situation gracefully, and probably all this does not mean anything more than that the dramatist has cast the Pages into roles they must play if he is to have a chance to develop his comic situation. For the moment at least, the spectator must close his character-eye and open his plot-eye, for the Elizabethan drama did not demand quite the character consistency which some critics would impose upon it.

9

to enforce the law, why did he not do it himself instead of leaving it to Angelo, whom he only half trusted? Why did he not know about Angelo's relations with Mariana? And once he had made up his mind what to do, why did he not tell Isabella the truth instead of torturing her with a cat-and-mouse game until the big revelation scene at the end of the play? The answer of course is that Shakespeare wanted the big revelation scene. He was writing a play, and other considerations must yield to the dramatic consideration. In *Romeo and Juliet* the faithful Friar runs off and leaves Juliet alone in the tomb with Romeo's body not because he is a coward but because she must have a chance to kill herself; otherwise the play will not be what the Elizabethans considered a tragedy. By the same token, Othello *must* believe Iago and Gloucester *must* be taken in by Edmund. Hamlet accepts his uncle's guilt at the beginning of the tragedy but does not kill him until the end because that was the way a revenge play had to be constructed; if he had killed him sooner, he would at the same time have killed the play.[4]

There are other, more difficult problems, however, and we may suspect that the Elizabethan audience could swallow some things that we cannot swallow. Romeo and Juliet kill themselves for love. Othello, misled by Iago's lying, slanderous tongue, kills Desdemona because he believes she has been unfaithful to him. And both Othello and the Veronese lovers are presented with great sympathy. Are we then to conclude that Shakespeare approved of love suicides and the slaughter of unfaithful wives?

Romeo and Juliet belongs to the secular bible of the Western world, and I have little doubt that there is more romantic love in that world than there would be if that play had never been written. Every now and then we still hear of a boy and girl stealing off to kill themselves for love, though I think we hear of it less often than we did a generation or two ago. It would not be difficult to convince me that some love suicides have been inspired by the Shakespearean example, but surely no normal person finds it at all difficult to sympathize with the two of Verona yet react to the

---

[4] This point is discussed further in my article "The Perfect Revenge—Hamlet's Delay: A Reconsideration," *College English*, X (1949), 188–95.

newspaper reports with anger, impatience, or at best a contemptuous sort of pity. What is the explanation? A simple one, I am persuaded. Romeo and Juliet are characters in a play, and that play is a romantic love tragedy. They have no reason for being except to be true to each other and to love until death. This they do superbly, and thus they win our admiration. But life is always much more complicated than art. Art simplifies, strips to essentials. More importantly, in the present connection, it eliminates considerations not germane to its immediate purpose. The youngsters who kill themselves today live (or refuse to live) in a much larger world than that of Romeo and Juliet. They have, or they ought to have, wider interests and obligations than those which claim Shakespeare's tragic characters. When they throw themselves away for love, we may therefore gravely suspect the existence of a mental disorder.[5]

Similar considerations apply to *Othello*, but the case is more complicated here. Though this play lacks the cosmic terror of

[5] It would, however, be a grave error to import such considerations as these into the evaluation of the play itself. The ultimate example of such foolishness was probably achieved by the nineteenth-century Hegelian, D. J. Snider. Convinced of the sanctity of the state and family and committed to a belief in poetic justice, Snider found himself obliged to prove that all Shakespeare's tragic heroes and heroines were quite as guilty as they were unfortunate. Thus Desdemona deserved her fate because she lied to Othello about the handkerchief, and the love of Romeo and Juliet was imperfect because they loved each other and were not devoted to the family as an institution! It is true that when Friar Laurence hears that Romeo has dropped Rosaline for Juliet he declares that "Young men's love then lies/ Not truly in their hearts, but in their eyes," making the familiar Elizabethan distinction between a superficial, sensual love, based on the fleeting attractions of the body, and a more profound spiritual love, rooted in the inward being of a man and a woman. But even Friar Laurence seems to change his mind about this as the play proceeds, and no reader has ever seen Romeo and Juliet as anything but utterly faithful lovers. As to the forces arrayed against them, which achieve their doom, these are neither state nor family as such but human stubbornness, wrong-headedness, and hatred. Because feuds between great families are no longer a live issue in modern society, modern productions of *Romeo and Juliet* used to drop the final curtain on the death of the lovers. Even Sothern and Marlowe did that; the first production of the play I ever saw which employed the ending Shakespeare intended was that of Katharine Cornell. I doubt that any intelligent producer would omit it today; if the long, moralizing wind-up strikes us as anticlimactic, it is still essential to the meaning of the drama. The lovers died because they eschewed hate and gave themselves to love, and their death becomes sacrificial and vicarious when it brings reconciliation to their families and peace to Verona.

King Lear, it is surely the most painful of all Shakespeare's tragedies, and so devoted a Shakespearean as Horace Howard Furness
declared roundly that he wished it had never been written. But
the nature of the problem may best be apprehended if we leave
Shakespeare for a moment to turn to an even more venerable
monument of our literature.

In Genesis 22 we read of Abraham's attempt to sacrifice his
son Isaac in obedience to God's command. The narrative moves,
with considerable detail, along a straight line of development,
until the boy has been bound upon the altar and Abraham reaches
forth his hand to slay him. Then the angel of the Lord calls to
him to forbid his proceeding further and to explain that God's
command was intended only as a test of his faith and loyalty, "for
now I know that thou fearest God, seeing thou hast not withheld
thy son, thine only son from me."

Because many people have the curious idea that it is not necessary to employ either their brains or their sensibilities when they
read the Bible, this story is often read by good Christians without
shock or any realization that it makes God a monster. There are
still people in the world unfortunately (I once knew one) who
sometimes get the idea that God wants them to sacrifice a child,
and who do it, in response to His supposed command. But we no
longer give them a high and holy place in sacred literature. Instead
we send them to the insane asylum. And nobody who reads admiringly the story of Abraham's attempt to sacrifice Isaac believes
we ought to do anything else.

Once more, the explanation is simple. The primitive Semitic
custom of sacrificing the first-born to the Deity no longer prevailed
when Genesis 22 was written. *But it was still a part of living
memory,* and in literature at least a sane man could entertain the
possibility of its being practiced under exceptional circumstances.
That day has passed. We still believe that a man's supreme loyalty
belongs to God (with whatever meaning we may choose to read
into that word), but a modern novelist or playwright devising a
test for a righteous man would never choose this one, for as soon

as his hero entertained any such idea, the audience would dismiss him as a criminal lunatic.[6]

Is it not very much the same with Othello's sacrifice? I am not saying that Elizabethans believed it to be "right" for a betrayed husband to slaughter his wife. I certainly am not saying that Shakespeare believed it, for unless I am completely wrong in my reading of his character, Shakespeare could not have deliberately killed any human being under any circumstances. But for literary-dramatic purposes, and in using a borrowed story, Shakespeare and his audience *could* conceive of such a situation and *could* present such a character sympathetically, though even here it may not be wholly accidental that Othello should have been not an Englishman nor even an Italian but a "Moor." Today, unless we go crazy first, we do not kill unfaithful wives or husbands but divorce them, and a modern playwright either could not use the Shakespearean situation or would handle it very differently. Surely all this shows a difference between Shakespeare's time and ours, perhaps even between Shakespeare and you or me. But just what that difference is it might be very difficult to spell out.[7]

There is one other thing which it would be well to keep in mind as we seek to discern Shakespeare in his plays, and this is that with him the dramatic interest, not the psychological and certainly not the confessional, is always paramount. Many matters are better motivated in his sources than they are in his plays, but his changes along this line increase the dramatic tension. It is a tribute to the extraordinary vitality of his characters that we should find it difficult to remember this; we must, however, make an effort to do so, for otherwise we shall seriously misinterpret both them and him. And again it may be well to begin with a very simple illustration.

At the end of Act I, Scene 1 of 1 *Henry IV*, Prince Hal informs the audience in a soliloquy that his association with thieves and

---

[6] It is also true unfortunately that we still sacrifice children (generally not to God but to the devil), but this is achieved in other ways and in any case is, as Kipling used to say, "another story."

[7] The Othello problem does not stand alone in Shakespeare. What shall be said of Posthumus, who, plotting the death of Imogen, does not even plan to kill her himself, but, like Achilles with his Myrmidons, turns the job over to another?

roisterers in London taverns represents only one stage in his life
and that when the proper time comes, he will stop sowing wild
oats and begin to reap tame ones:

> I know you all, and will a while uphold
> The unyok'd humour of your idleness.
> Yet herein will I imitate the sun,
> Who doth permit the base contagious clouds
> To smother up his beauty from the world,
> That when he please again to be himself
> Being wanted, he may be more wond'red at
> By breaking through the foul and ugly mists
> Of vapours that did seem to strangle him.
> If all the year were playing holidays,
> To sport would be as tedious as to work;
> But when they seldom come, they wish'd for come,
> And nothing pleaseth but rare accidents.
> So, when this loose behaviour I throw off
> And pay the debt I never promised,
> By how much better than my word I am,
> By so much shall I falsify men's hopes;
> And like bright metal on a sullen ground,
> My reformation, glitt'ring o'er my fault,
> Shall show more goodly and attract more eyes
> Than that which hath no foil to set it off.
> I'll so offend to make offence a skill,
> Redeeming time when men think least I will.

Psychologically this is quite unbelievable. It seems safe to say that
no young man in history ever sowed wild oats for any such motive
as is here alleged. But it does not follow, as Quiller-Couch believed, that Shakespeare intended us to think of the Prince as "a
prig of a rake"; neither are we to search for some failing in the
dramatist to explain why he did not know that such a rake was
detestable. The purpose of the soliloquy is to clear the Prince, not
blacken him. His roistering and his reformation were both inherited from the chronicles. Shakespeare could not have avoided

using these elements, and he certainly would not have wished to do so, for in order to achieve this, he would have been obliged to sacrifice Falstaff. There was nothing for it save to adhere to the familiar outlines of the accepted story and at the same time put an exculpating speech into the Prince's mouth. Shakespeare could not have caused another character to speak for Hal, for nobody was in his confidence to the required extent. His soliloquy therefore was quite as formal as the "balloons" which emerge from the mouths of the figures in some old tapestries to proclaim that "I am the mighty conqueror," etc., and quite as much supposed to be taken at face value. It "keeps the Prince from appearing vile in the opinion of the audience." You are not supposed to consider it critically; you are supposed to accept it.

There are other cases, however, where the issue may not at first seem quite so clear. "I have given suck," says Lady Macbeth,

> and know
> How tender 'tis to love the babe that milks me;
> I would, while it was smiling in my face,
> Have pluck'd my nipple from his boneless gums
> And dash'd the brains out, had I so sworn as you
> Have done to this.

No children of the Macbeths appear or are anywhere referred to elsewhere in the play. "He has no children," cries Macduff, after his own have been slaughtered, by way of explaining why the "revenge" which Malcolm urges upon him is not feasible, and this is suitable, for monsters should not have children.[8] If Lady Macbeth ever had a child, therefore, it must be dead. But here, according to some interpreters, Shakespeare adds a dimension to his portrait of the "fiend-like queen"; if her children had lived, the womanly side of her nature might have developed, etc.; to all of which it does not seem necessary to say anything more than that it is not the Shakespearean method to characterize thus by half-hidden touches. If he had thought of Lady Macbeth as a child-

[8] It does not of course follow that if Macbeth had had children, Macduff would have proceeded to slaughter them, though learned critical craniums have been troubled about that too!

starved woman, he would have found some means of telling us so; as Kittredge says, "nothing that is omitted is of any significance."[9] Shakespeare wrote for a popular audience, not for devotees of the avant-garde or the implicational. Lady Macbeth never speaks of her motherhood except in this scene, and her statement was not intended to carry elaborate implications for the play as a whole. She is inciting her husband to murder, and Shakespeare needs the strongest possible statement he can find to put into her mouth. Women do have children. Women suckle children and love them, and a woman who will brutally murder her child will do anything that is evil. Of course it is not necessary to suppose that Lady Macbeth would actually have done what she says; she speaks in the heat of argument. But her statement shocks the audience beyond anything else Shakespeare could have had her say. Once it had achieved that purpose, he was through with it. It was again the choice of the dramatic as against the purely psychological effect. It would be ridiculous to suppose that having given Lady Macbeth children in this speech, Shakespeare must have kept that fact in mind throughout the tragedy that she had had children and modified or developed his conception of her character accordingly. Some modern writers, more likely to be novelists than playwrights, might have done just that. But not Shakespeare. Elizabethan dramatists did not go in for quite that kind of consistency.[10]

We make fun of the nineteenth-century ladies who wrote essays on such subjects as "the girlhood of Shakespeare's heroines." Shakespeare's heroines had no girlhood. They were born when they stepped on the stage, and they ceased to exist when the play was over. But though this objection is well taken, we are no better than the nineteenth-century critics when we speculate concerning the circumstances of King Lear's married life and wonder whether

[9] George Lyman Kittredge, *Shakspere* (HUP, 1916), 15.

[10] When Juliet (III, 3:116ff.) says that it would have been better to hear that both her parents were dead rather than Romeo banished, we are not to conclude that she hated her parents (though she might certainly have had good excuse!) nor that she was an undutiful daughter. Shakespeare is simply giving the strongest emphasis possible to her love for Romeo.

his relations with his late wife contributed to the situation which exists at the beginning of the play, or even whether Cordelia was to blame for refusing to flatter her father, thus turning him over to the tender mercies of her sisters, or whether there was any justification for the complaints made by Goneril and Regan concerning the behavior of Lear's knights. Gordon Bottomley probably did not intend to be taken quite seriously when he wrote *King Lear's Wife*, but there have been others who have approached such matters without humor, grace, or imagination.[11] Nor will it do to accuse Shakespeare of political naïveté because he presents Lear, at the beginning of the play, as dividing up his kingdom. Of course Shakespeare knew that no real king could possibly do such a thing. If possible, he knew it even better than we do, for the horror of the Roses was not yet forgotten in Elizabethan England. But Lear was not a real king but a stage king, once more in an inherited story. The situation presented is a "just suppose" situation. We are no more called upon to sit through the performance debating in our minds whether or not the initial act could have happened than we find it necessary to sit through *Peter Pan* wondering whether we believe in fairies.[12] It does happen. We have seen it happen. But it happens on the stage. Suppose it did happen. What would follow? That is what the play is about.

These, then, are the danger signals I think it well to post at the beginning of our journey. Some may feel that I have made what was already a sufficiently dangerous quest seem nearly desperate. But let us not yet despair.

[11] As, for example, by P. Fijn van Draat, whose "King Lear and his Daughters," *Englische Studien*, LXXX (1936), 352–57, and "King Lear," *Anglia*, LXI (1937), 177–85, are excellent examples of how not to do it. In *The Truth about Shylock* (Random House, 1962), Bernard Grebanier records an extreme example of the confusion between literature and life in considering Shakespearean matters. When Maurice Schwartz dramatized *Shylock and his Daughter* from a novel by Ari Ibn Zahav, he professed to show "the real Shylock." The implication must be that Shakespeare's was a false Shylock, yet it is only in Shakespeare's play that Shylock ever existed.

[12] Barrie, one of the canniest of dramatists, tricked his doubting audience by forcing it to testify to its belief in fairies by applauding to save Tinker Bell's life. He knew that once you have done something about a belief, it is pretty fairly grounded. If Shakespeare never goes to this length, the reason may be that he was writing in a less skeptical age.

II

THE GREAT GLOBE ITSELF

John Aubrey, writing about 1681, and echoing the actor William Beeston, calls Shakespeare "a handsome, well-shap't man." The portraits with the best claim to authenticity are the bust at Stratford and the engraving by Martin Droeshout in the First Folio; unfortunately both are such inferior art works that we cannot feel safe in relying upon them implicitly. Nevertheless, the domelike, partly bald head and the somewhat bulging forehead probably reflect actuality. The Stratford bust gives him auburn hair and large hazel eyes, but this coloring is modern. The Chandos portrait is much more attractive, but it may have been idealized.

Though a country boy, Shakespeare was far from being the "peasant" the Baconians like to call him, for his father was one of the leading citizens of Stratford. It is true that he early suffered reverses the nature of which we do not clearly understand, but this does not seem to have altered the esteem in which his fellow townsmen held him. Shakespeare's country boyhood was important for his creative sensitivity and perhaps for his health, about which we really know nothing except what may be inferred

from his references to disease and healing.[1] But an indoor play like *Othello* is an anomaly with Shakespeare; his customary theater is the green earth beneath and the blue sky above him, with winds and clouds and sea and shore, and inhabited not only by multitudinous human beings but by a wide variety of furred and feathered creatures, and supernatural beings also when he needed them. If his years in London added much to his interior climate, his imagery does not show it. He never cut the ties to his home base at Stratford, and as soon as it became possible, he returned there to stay.

Perhaps *A Midsummer Night's Dream*—in which somebody has counted forty-two varieties of flowers, trees, and shrubs—*As You Like It*, and *The Winter's Tale* are generally thought of as the plays in which he made the richest use of his country boyhood, but they certainly do not stand alone. He knew the glories of sunrise (though they were not always benevolent)—

> Once more the ruby-colour'd portal open'd,
> Which to his speech did honey passage yield;
> Like a red morn, that ever yet betoken'd
> Wreck to the seaman, tempest to the field,
>   Sorrow to shepherds, woe unto the birds,
>   Gusts and foul flaws to herdsmen and to herds—

and of sunset and the drawing in of night—

> "Look, the world's comforter with weary gait
> His day's hot task hath ended in the west;
> The owl, night's herald, shrieks; 'tis very late;
> The sheep are gone to fold, birds to their nest;

---

[1] See Alban Doran's account of Elizabethan medicine in *Shakespeare's England* (OUP, 1916) and the more popular "Medical Report" in Ivor Brown, *How Shakespeare Spent the Day* (Hill and Wang, 1963). Edgar I. Fripp, *Shakespeare, Man and Artist* (OUP, 1938), 691 ff., considers Shakespeare's knowledge of medicine, and Caroline F. E. Spurgeon, *Shakespeare's Imagery and What It Teaches Us* (M, 1935), 129ff., contains a suggestive analysis of his images of sickness and medicine. Miss Spurgeon believes that Shakespeare was interested in medicine all his life and that this interest increased as he grew older, also that he was far "ahead of his time in such questions as the relation of temperate living to health. . . ."

And coal-black clouds that shadow heaven's light
Do summon us to part and bid good-night."[2]

Clouds interest both Hamlet and Antony for the fantastic shapes they can assume, and the sea is often associated with danger and mystery, but the inroads of the waves upon the shore suggest the triumph of time, which Shakespeare refers to in other connections again and again:

Like as the waves make towards the pebbled shore,
So do our minutes hasten to their end.[3]

There are many references to gardening,[4] and in *Richard II* (III, 4) a garden symbolizes the commonwealth.

Bradley finds[5] the rose and the lily the flowers most frequently spoken of in Shakespeare, but with the fragrance of the violet even more heavily stressed than that of the rose. Judged by modern standards, there is no minute notation of either fauna or flora, but the marigold in Sonnet 25 is interesting. Imogen has on her breast

A mole cinque-spotted, like the crimson drops
I' the bottom of a cowslip.

Ophelia distributes various flowers during her mad scene, and Perdita is specific enough about

[2] Both quotations are from *Venus and Adonis*.

[3] David Masson, *Shakespeare Personally* (Du, 1914) comments on "the fixed or ever-recurring idea [in the Sonnets] of Death, Change, Mortality, Time, the merely phantasmagoric character of all that now is and glitters so bravely as our mundane round of things, the fated march of all toward extinction and evanescence, that idea which we averred might be chased all through Shakespeare's plays, and to which he gave such marvellous utterance in that burst of Prospero's in *The Tempest*." See also a more recent, much more thoroughgoing and far-reaching discussion by Frederick Turner, *Shakespeare and the Nature of Time: Moral and Philosophical Themes in Some Plays and Poems of William Shakespeare* (OUP, 1971).

[4] See Fripp, 467ff. and the many references to gardens and gardening in Spurgeon. One of the liveliest things in Miss Spurgeon's book is her account of how she discovered that a water passage in *The Rape of Lucrece* was based on Shakespeare's remembrance of the movement of the Avon at Clopton Bridge. See her frontispiece and pp. 96–98.

[5] A. C. Bradley, "Shakespeare the Man" in *Oxford Lectures on Poetry* (M, 1909).

> our carnations and streak'd gillyflowers,
> Which some call Nature's bastards,

and again about

> bold oxlips
> The crown imperial; lilies of all kinds,
> The flower-de-luce being one!

but it is not for such things that one remembers her but rather for her breath-taking references to

> daffodils
> That come before the swallow dares, and take
> The winds of March with beauty

and the

> pale primroses,
> That die unmarried, ere they can behold
> Bright Phoebus in his strength.

Shakespeare was always ready to praise "earth's increase, foison plenty," but he was no more a botanist in his references to flowers than he was a geographer when he gave Bohemia a seacoast. *As You Like It* is supposed to take place in France, but if Shakespeare had any definite locality in mind while writing the play, it must have been his own Warwickshire, yet he introduces animals which could be found neither in France nor in England. M. M. Reese was therefore quite right when he remarked that although Shakespeare "was pre-eminently the poet of Nature and the countryside, drawing on them for a ceaseless flow of imagery that never fails to touch the heart," he was interested in nature not for its own sake "but only as it prompted him to reflection on the ways of men."[6] In *As You Like It*, again, the banished Duke finds moral meanings in nature,

---

[6] *Shakespeare, His World and His Work* (A, 1953). Reese also makes the interesting suggestion that solitude did not please Shakespeare; "whenever he bids us accompany him to forest or island, it is because men are living there." But how could he write a play otherwise?

> tongues in trees, books in the running brooks,
> Sermons in stones, and good in every thing.

This point of view is not uncharacteristic of Shakespeare, but it does not strike his dominant note. Though he was always interested in what nature "means," he was never concerned to impose meaning upon her.

A *Midsummer Night's Dream* adds fairy splendor to natural beauty, and Titania sends her fairies

> Some to kill cankers in the musk-rose buds,
> Some war with rere-mice for their leathern wings
> To make my small elves coats, and some keep back
> The clamorous owl that nightly hoots and wonders
> At our quaint spirits.

When she is enamored of Bottom she commands them to

> Hop in his walks and gambol in his eyes;
> Feed him with apricocks and dewberries,
> With purple grapes, green figs, and mulberries;
> The honey-bags steal from the humble bees,
> And for night-tapers crop their waxen thighs
> And light them at the fiery glow-worm's eyes,
> To have my love to bed and to arise;
> And pluck the wings from painted butterflies
> To fan the moonbeams from his sleeping eyes.

Arthur Rackham was the best illustrator the *Dream* ever had, or ever will have,[7] and it is not surprising that it should be difficult to say whether he has been more successful in depicting the fairies or the beauties of the English countryside, for the two elements can hardly be separated in the play itself. Nor need we be surprised that the dramatist should be willing to place the "unnatural natural history" he inherited from the Middle Ages side by side

---

[7] There are two entirely separate editions by Rackham, one published by Heinemann, 1908, and the other by The Limited Editions Club, 1939. The New York Public Library has a third set of, presumably, unpublished illustrations, which I have not seen.

with his own first-hand observation. But the imaginative note is always more characteristic in Shakespeare than the merely fanciful. Nature and human nature are one in Sonnet 33:

Full many a glorious morning have I seen
Flatter the mountain tops with sovereign eye,
Kissing with golden face the meadows green,
Gilding pale streams with heavenly alchemy;
Anon permit the basest clouds to ride
With ugly rack on his celestial face,
And from the forlorn world his visage hide,
Stealing unseen to west with this disgrace.

In another even more imaginative sonnet (97)—"How like a winter hath my absence been"—a personal relationship is presented in terms of the cycle of the year.

Close to the enjoyment of nature lies hunting, swimming, and various other outdoor sports: archery, football, tennis, wrestling, bowls, and billiards (the last oddly, and I should think anachronistically, one of Cleopatra's pastimes in Egypt).[8] Bassanio risks another arrow to find a lost one, and Benvolio assures Romeo that a right fair mark is soonest hit. Wrestling is important in the plot of *As You Like It,* and Touchstone shows himself more sensitive than many moderns when he expresses amazement that the breaking of ribs should be sport for ladies. In *Henry V* the Dauphin expresses his contempt for the English king by sending him tennis balls, but the Dauphin is himself a fribble, as his silly attitude toward his horse (III, 7) is soon to show. Among indoor amusements, dancing is of course a fixed part of the social scene, and Romeo and Juliet meet at a ball. The addle-pated Sir Andrew Aguecheek delights in masques and revels, "sometimes altogether." Games no longer familiar to us are sometimes mentioned: wild goose chase; tick-tack; and hide, fox, and all after. There is very little said about cards, the most interesting reference being in

---

[8] Miss Spurgeon found three times as many references to bowling in Shakespeare as to any other game; she found little interest in fishing. On sports in general, see, further, Fripp, 385ff. As always, *Shakespeare's England* (OUP, 1916) is valuable for backgrounds.

3 Henry VI (V, 1:44)—"The king was slily finger'd from the deck"—which was once used to prove to an English scholar that "deck" for "pack" was not an Americanism, as he had supposed, but an American survival from older English usage. The worst gamester in Shakespeare is the unspeakable Cloten of *Cymbeline*, whose debauched ways are no testimonial for the pursuit.

Shakespeare often associates both wild and tame animals with stock characteristics—as when Albany calls Lear's wicked daughters tigers. There are three famous references to the lark: the song "Hark, hark the lark" in *Cymbeline*; the passage in *Venus and Adonis* which begins, "Lo, here the gentle lark," and which to us seems a song also since Bishop's musical setting of it is as familiar as what Schubert did for the other piece; and in Sonnet 29 the presentation of the poet's state as "like to the lark at break of day arising." Beatrice in *Much Ado* runs along the ground like a lapwing, and there are a number of bird references in *Macbeth*. Arriving at Inverness, the doomed King Duncan is charmed by the martins nesting there.

> Where they [most] breed and haunt, I have obser'vd
> The air is delicate.[9]

Later, Lady Macduff, also unwittingly facing death, speaks of the brave defense of that "most diminutive of birds," the wren, against the owl who would invade her nest. But for Macbeth himself even birds share in the horror with which his crime has impregnated the whole of life.

> Light thickens, and the crow
> Makes wing to th' rooky wood;
> Good things of day begin to droop and drowse,
> And night's black agents to their preys do rouse.

There are more references to falcons (and to hawking), however,

---

[9] Cf. Bernard Shaw's use of the martins in his hilarious rewriting of the last act of *Macbeth* in the style of a novel "By Arnold Bennett, John Galsworthy, or Anybody"—"Mr. Arnold Bennett Thinks Playwriting Easier than Novel Writing," *Pen Portraits and Reviews*, "Ayot St. Lawrence Edition, The Collected Works of Bernard Shaw," Vol. XXIX (Wm. H. Wise & Company, 1932).

than to any other bird, and these are not always given to characters who might normally be expected to speak of such matters. Juliet longs

> for a falconer's voice,
> To lure this tassel-gentle back again!

The tortured Othello vows that once he is sure that Desdemona is "haggard,"

> Though that her jesses were my dear heartstrings,
> I'd whistle her off and let her down the wind
> To prey at fortune.

In *Venus and Adonis*, the falcon

> tow'ring in the skies,
> Coucheth the fowl below with his wings' shade.[10]

And in *Macbeth*, again, where all nature is turned upside down by sin,

> On Tuesday last,
> A falcon, tow'ring in her pride of place,
> Was by a mousing owl hawk'd at and kill'd.

Horses and dogs get more attention from Shakespeare than any other animals, but this is mainly in connection with hunting. I do not find that he had any interest in pet dogs. Launce's dog in *The Two Gentlemen of Verona* is pretty stock, and Cordelia's

> Mine enemy's dog,
> Though he had bit me, should have stood that night
> Against my fire

shows her kindness of heart, not the worthiness of the creature,

---

[10] James Russell Lowell commented upon this ("Spenser," *Among My Books*) as an example of Shakespeare's inevitable dramatizing, his passing from simple sensation to meaning. "The sun 'flatters the mountain-tops with sovereign eye'; the bending weeds 'lacquey the dull stream'; the shadow of the falcon 'coucheth the fowl below'; the smoke is 'helpless'; when Tarquin enters the chamber of Lucrece 'the threshold grates the door to have him heard.' "

though perhaps a little more intimacy may be claimed for Lear's own

The little dogs and all,
Tray, Blanch, and Sweetheart, see, they bark at me.[11]

Portia does not relish the "horsy" Neapolitan prince among her suitors. Baptista's servant Biondello rattles off what is almost a catalogue of equine diseases in his report concerning the steed upon which Petruchio approaches to his wedding, and Richard II uses his lost Barbary as a hook upon which to hang his sentimental embroidery, precisely as he uses everything else. The most detailed notation of animal behavior in Shakespeare, however, is that of the amorous courser in *Venus and Adonis*, though one must admit that this is almost rivaled by the boar and hare in the same poem, both of them animals the poet could not possibly have known nearly so well. That he did know horses there can be no doubt, however; even Ariel shares this knowledge, though one must wonder where he acquired it. "Then I beat my tabor," he tells Prospero, reporting the tactics employed upon the enemy,

At which, like unback'd colts, they prick'd their ears,
Advanc'd their eyelids, lifted up their noses
As they smelt music.

That the passages I have quoted—and many more I have had no space to quote—were written by a man unfamiliar with the sights and sounds of the hunting field I think few readers will believe, but what Shakespeare's attitude toward all this may have been is not so easy to formulate. If only Jaques of *As You Like It* and the Shepherd of *The Winter's Tale* seem actually opposed to hunting,[12] there is no denying that Shakespeare's hunting scenes often

[11] Spurgeon, 195–99, comments upon the curious association in Shakespearean imagery of "dog or spaniel, fawning and licking; candy, sugar or sweets, thawing or melting." She suggests that the fastidious Shakespeare was revolted by the feeding of dogs while the family sat at meat and that the disgust thus engendered may have extended to the animals themselves.

[12] The old story that Shakespeare was driven from Stratford after a poaching expedition in Sir Thomas Lucy's preserves has been rejected by nearly all careful scholars not because it is inherently improbable but simply because we have no

focus on the hunted rather than the hunters, and this is the more impressive because he is so obviously not feeding out propaganda in defense of a preformulated attitude but merely expressing, perhaps even half-unconsciously, his own natural feelings. The description of the hare in Venus and Adonis, already referred to, is a good example; more remarkable still, since it refers to the sufferings of a creature with which most men have not sufficient imagination to feel empathy, is that of the wounded snail:

> Or, as the snail, whose tender horns being hit,
> Shrinks backward in his shelly cave with pain,
> And there, all smother'd up, in shade doth sit,
> Long after fearing to creep forth again;
>> So, at his bloody view, her eyes are fled
>> Into the deep-dark cabins of her head.

More unusual still is the business about the fly in Titus Andronicus (III, 2), which it must be difficult for any modern reader to encounter without recalling the wonderful story by Katherine Mansfield.

One of Shakespeare's characters is permitted to recognize and refer to the phenomenon of ailurophobia ("some, that are mad if they behold a cat"). Shylock himself does not seem to have been an ailurophobe, however, for he goes on to speak of Pussy as both "harmless" and "necessary." It was different with Bertram of All's Well That Ends Well, who is the worst cat-hater in Shakespeare ("I could endure anything before but a cat; and now he's a cat to me"). Iago is in character when he advises Roderigo to "drown cats and blind puppies," and Falstaff of The Merry Wives has a reference to drowning "a blind bitch's puppies, fifteen in the litter." The truth is there are no really friendly references to cats in Shakespeare, and it seems clear that he did not like them. There are some neutral references to the cat's mousing prowess (this was probably the ground on which Shylock called her

evidence which makes it seem reasonable to believe that the incident ever occurred. Perhaps the most cogent and comprehensive argument against it is that of John Semple Smart, Shakespeare, Truth and Tradition Chapter IV—"Things That Never Were" (A, 1928).

"necessary") and her fondness for milk (Falstaff calls himself "as vigilant as a cat to steal cream"), but the only one of these in which the imagination seems really caught up is in the Prologue to Act III of *Pericles*, which may be non-Shakespearean:

> The cat, with eyne of burning coal,
> Now couches ['fore] the mouse's hole.

In *Macbeth* the cat is associated conventionally with witchcraft, and Lady Macbeth, goading her husband to murder, taunts him with being "like the poor cat i' the adage," whose desire for fish was not strong enough to persuade her to get her feet wet. Benedick is probably thinking of the agonies which medieval superstitions caused to be inflicted upon cats when he offers, in case he should fall in love, to permit himself to be hung up in a bottle and shot at "like a cat." All the other references, I think, are hostile. Stephano calls Caliban a cat, and Volumnia calls the Roman rabble cats. Hermia clinging unwanted to Lysander is called both cat and serpent, and Hamlet puts gib with bat and paddock. But the worst cat reference in Shakespeare, and surely one of the worst in literature, occurs in *The Rape of Lucrece*, where the rapist Tarquin is called "foul night-walking cat."

Since England is not a particularly serpent-infested country, Shakespeare seems to have a rather surprisingly large number of references to snakes, the adder, I think, being the only particular variety mentioned. Only one passage in *Venus and Adonis* specifically mentions snake-fear—what Emily Dickinson calls "zero at the bone":

> By this, she hears the hounds are at a bay;
> Whereat she starts, like one that spies an adder
> Wreath'd up in fatal folds just in his way,
> The fear whereof doth make him shake and shudder;
>   Even so the timorous yelping of the hounds
>   Appalls her senses and her spirit confounds.

Nevertheless, most of Shakespeare's ophidian references associate the snake with horror, evil, and malevolence, sometimes alone and

sometimes in association with such creatures as toads, lizards, and spiders. According to the Ghost of the elder Hamlet, the murderer Claudius circulated the rumor that he had died of snakebite, but this was of course not true. In A *Midsummer Night's Dream* Hermia dreams of being menaced by a snake, and in *As You Like It* Orlando saves his wicked brother from one. Snakes are associated with witchcraft in *Macbeth*, and the king himself uses snake symbolism when speaking of his fear of Banquo. Juliet is afraid of serpents; Aufidius in *Coriolanus* speaks of hating them in Africa; Richard II refers to St. Patrick's service in driving them out of Ireland. Rosalind contemptuously calls the love-sick Silvius "a tame snake," and *Titus Andronicus* has references to a starved snake in need of water and a snake lying rolled "in the cheerful sun." Snakes are prominently associated with Egypt in *Antony and Cleopatra*, and Cleopatra revels in the pet name Antony gave her—"my serpent of old Nile." Though she chooses at last to die by snakebite, there are several passages, especially in Act II, Scene 4, where she, too, associates horror and malignity with the creatures. The horrible passage in *2 Henry VI* in which

> the snake roll'd in a flow'ring bank,
> With shining checker'd slough, doth sting a child
> That for the beauty thinks it excellent

may not be Shakespearean, but A *Midsummer Night's Dream* does not fit completely into the pattern which seems to be emerging. In this play, too, the dominant tone of the ophidian references is unpleasant, for even the fairy song, though beautiful and gentle, serves notice on the creatures that they are not welcome:

> You spotted snakes with double tongue,
>   Thorny hedgehogs, be not seen;
> Newts and blind-worms, do no wrong,
>   Come not near our fairy queen.

On the other hand, Oberon tells Robin Goodfellow that by the "bank where the wild thyme blows,"

> the snake throws her enamell'd skin
> Weed wide enough to wrap a fairy in,

which is hardly the utterance of a thoroughgoing snake-hater.

III

THE WORLD WITHIN
THE MIND

I

However sensitive a great poet may be to either the beauties or the horrors of the world around him, these things are primarily important as raw materials for his creativity in the world that lives inside his skull. We must not place too much emphasis upon Ben Jonson's statement that Shakespeare had little Latin and less Greek, for Ben almost thought in Latin, and he could be very grand about such things. Of Holofernes and Sir Nathaniel Shakespeare tells us in *Love's Labour's Lost* that "they have been at a great feast of languages, and stol'n the scraps," and he was certainly capable of a similar feat when it suited his ends. William Beeston, the actor, told Aubrey that Shakespeare was a schoolteacher in the country during his so-called "lost" years (1584–92), and Chambers and Adams have certainly made this seem a more reasonable hypothesis than some of the more picturesque guesses which have attached themselves to this period.[1] As for the modern

[1] There are useful studies of Shakespeare's Latin learning by Fripp, 114ff. and by John Semple Smart, *op. cit.* Among recent writers, Fripp makes the most determined case for Shakespeare's having spent a period in a lawyer's office, which is argued on the ground of his familiarity with legal terminology, which, Fripp

languages, it is not always possible to tell whether he used a foreign source directly or in translation, but it must be admitted that those who are bound to have him an ignorant man at any cost have been driven to some pretty desperate expedients, as, for example, hypothesizing him to have seen a translation in manuscript before it was published in order to prove their case.

Whatever the adequacy or inadequacy of Shakespeare's education may have been, it was of course a literary, not a scientific, education. We have already noted his interest in medicine, and astronomy and navigation are both involved in the great Sonnet 114, yet Shakespeare seems to me to have been less interested in science than Chaucer had been so long before him.

There are also some interesting references to astrology, which was in as good repute in Elizabethan times as astronomy is now. Helena discusses it with Parolles in *All's Well* (I, 1), but her conclusion seems to be that

> Our remedies oft in ourselves do lie,
> Which we ascribe to heaven,

which is exactly the point of the "dear Brutus" speech in *Julius Caesar* which gave Barrie the title for one of his best plays. Later, however, she attributes her condition to an "ill planet" and resolves to be patient till the heavens change. Polonius warns Ophelia that Prince Hamlet is "out of thy star," and Romeo and Juliet are "star-cross'd lovers." When he hears of Juliet's supposed death, Romeo defies the stars, but the results of this defiance are not happy; dying, he shakes "the yoke of inauspicious stars" from his "world-wearied" flesh.[2] Iago, reporting to Othello the fight in

---

thought, he often used figuratively and in unexpected connections. "We cannot claim for Shakespeare profound legal knowledge; he was not a barrister or counsellor, but a country lawyer he certainly was." But "certainly" is certainly too strong. Smart raises the possibility of his having spent some time at Oxford during his "lost" years. This is certainly not incredible, but we have no evidence to support the hypothesis, as Smart himself realized.

[2] See in this connection John W. Draper's article, "Shakespeare's Star-Crossed Lovers," *Review of English Studies*, XV (1939), 16–34. Though Draper seems to ride his astrological horse pretty hard, his accumulation of lore is impressive; if Shakespeare cannot be supposed to have had all of it in mind, he lived in the

which Cassio has disgraced himself, half professes to believe that "some planet had outwitted men," but he is probably no more sincere here than he is anywhere else. There can be no question that Lear's Kent believes devoutly in astrology, and though his villainous son Edmund rejects everything that suggests superstition, he rejects everything that has to do with religion along with it. I do not believe, as many have believed, that Prospero represents Shakespeare, but surely the dramatist never created a character he presented more admiringly, and he did not scruple to make Prospero say that he brought his enemies to the island because

> I find my zenith doth depend upon
> A most auspicious star, whose influence
> If I now court not but but omit, my fortunes
> Will ever after droop.

Psychology in the modern sense Shakespeare could not know, and we cannot be sufficiently thankful for what he escaped, for his ignorance left him free to make use of everything that his keen intelligence and observation could teach him about human nature but never tempted him to force preconceived patterns upon it. If King Duncan speaks for him, he took no stock in Renaissance notions about physiognomy: "There's no art/ To find the mind's construction in the face." The Nurse's chatter in *Romeo and Juliet* shows that he had marked the complete lack of selectivity which occurs in ignorant, talkative people. He understood the irrational mixture of love and hatred in Cloten's feeling for Imogen and saw King Leontes' jealousy as disease. Macbeth asked his wife's doctor for what we should now call psychosomatic medicine.

Perhaps the most interesting item under this heading is Ophelia's singing of bawdy songs during her mad scene. The

world of which it was a part, and he may well have been familiar with some of it. I would say very much the same thing about many other studies of Elizabethan intellectual backgrounds, including Lily B. Campbell, *Shakespeare's Tragic Heroes, Slaves of Passion* (CUP, 1930) and Walter Clyde Curry, *Shakespeare's Philosophical Patterns*, Second Edition (Louisiana State University Press, 1959).

learned have often misunderstood this, and we have been told that Shakespeare was trying to tell the audience that Ophelia had had sexual experience with Hamlet. Getting a thing exactly wrong is only less difficult than getting it exactly right (as the saying is, even a stopped clock is right twice every day), but here it has triumphantly been achieved. It is the normally suppressed part of the personality that expresses itself in insanity or delirium. I do not know how Shakespeare found that out, but he knew. There was not much about human nature that he did not know. Yet the general tone of the mad scene is nonrealistic and ballad-like. All the pathos of insanity is here; everything that is disgusting has been banished. Even Ophelia's suicide (if it was suicide) is, as the Queen describes it, beautiful. "The immodesty of . . . these songs," said Henry N. Hudson long ago, "is surpassingly touching; it tells us, as nothing else could, that Ophelia is utterly unconscious of what she is saying."

Was Shakespeare a reading man, a lover of books? Very little is said about his characters' reading, though both Hamlet and Ophelia use books as props. In the horrific *Titus Andronicus*, which is by all means the most literary play that has been attributed to Shakespeare, the unfortunate Lavinia, who, in happier days, had read "sweet poetry and Tully's Orator" (Cicero's *De Oratore*) with young Lucius, reveals the outrage which has been committed upon her by opening the *Metamorphoses* to the tragic story of Philomel. Brutus reads for a little before Philippi, and Imogen is, I think, the only heroine we ever see reading anything more than a letter, or, in Rosalind's case, one of Orlando's poems, which she has plucked off a tree. Imogen reads in bed, preparing herself for sleep the night Iachimo conceals himself in her chamber, and I cannot refrain from expressing the horror which I am sure every librarian in the country will share with me that both she and Brutus turn down the leaf to mark their places! (Did Shakespeare, then, set the example, here also?)

As for Shakespeare himself, if he was not a bookish writer in the sense of using many literary allusions, his range of references is sufficiently wide to prove that if he did not always read intensively,

he did read widely. Certainly he did not confine himself to what were, in the narrower sense of the term, literary works, as we ought to have realized from the fact that he used Plutarch and Holinshed not only in his historical plays but also in such tragedies as *Macbeth*, *Antony and Cleopatra*, and *Coriolanus*. Frank Kermode judges him "a strong-minded, wilful, private, reading man," and catches glimpses of him

> looking through books on Popish impostures, on the law of honour, on travel, on history, on law. He must have read deeper in Holinshed than his plots required, and gone into Plutarch beyond the plots he was using. He knew something of the commentators on Terence; he knew Palingenius, emblem books, and of course the Bible.[3]

Certainly he did not neglect contemporary literature. He was influenced by the current popularity of the tragedy of blood (whose type play was Kyd's *Spanish Tragedy*) early in his career and perhaps by the Beaumont-Fletcher type of dramatic romance toward the close. Daniel may well have influenced the Sonnets and *Henry IV*. Sidney is quoted in *The Merry Wives of Windsor* and Marlowe both here and in *As You Like It*, where Rabelais is also referred to. Lyly's Euphuism hovers in the background of both *Henry IV* and *Love's Labour's Lost*, and what was then the contemporary novel yielded the plots of *As You Like It* and *The Winter's Tale*. Like Chaucer and other great writers, Shakespeare never made books a substitute for life, but he did use them as an added dimension of life. And when he turned from written records, he turned not only to the life of his own day but to the whole world of folklore, popular superstition, and oral tradition besides—Robin Hood and Maid Marian, Queen Mab, Robin Goodfellow and the fairies, the balladry of the rogue Autolycus and Mamilius' tales for winter—and all this is a large part of his charm.

What, if anything, did Shakespeare draw from music and the plastic arts? Reese thinks that "architecture meant little to him

[3] *Shakespeare, Spenser, Donne: Renaissance Essays* (VP, 1971), 183, 199.

and he expected painting to be merely photographic," which last seems a rather anachronistic form of reference. The "painted cloths" he often refers to—a kind of middle-class substitute for tapestries—he may well have become acquainted with in his own home. Julio Romano is the only contemporary artist named (in *The Winter's Tale*). *The Rape of Lucrece* has an extremely elaborate description of

> a piece
> Of skilful painting, made for Priam's Troy;
> Before the which is drawn the power of Greece
> For Helen's rape the city to destroy.

This seems to me to be done in purely literary and dramatic terms, but as readers of my appendix will discover, Manly discovered much more than that in it.

On the other hand, I should suppose Shakespeare to have had considerable interest in music. The Elizabethan theater made much freer use of both music and dancing than the "legitimate" modern drama does, and since Shakespeare was an actor he may very well have sung upon the stage. Many delightful songs are scattered through the plays, and what we might call "mood music" is used by Portia in Bassanio's casket scene (some have even believed that the song to which Bassanio listened may have suggested the right choice), by Cleopatra, and by Duke Orsino of *Twelfth Night*, whose preference is for "an old and antique song," and who, in his most sentimental mood, deliberately steeps himself in music. Bradley thought Shakespeare stressed the "softening, tranquillising, or pensive influence" of music, but he also cited the peculiar statement of the Duke in *Measure for Measure* that music has "a charm/ To make bad good and good provoke to harm" and Cleopatra's description of music as "moody food/ Of us that trade in love," which perhaps attributes an aphrodisiac power to music, though Bradley does not say so. We have bird song in *The Rape of Lucrece* and music of supernatural origin when Antony's god leaves him in *Antony and Cleopatra* (IV, 4). Music inspires melancholy in Jaques ("I can suck melancholy out

of a song as a weasel sucks eggs") and apparently in Lorenzo's Jessica ("I am never merry when I hear sweet music"), but to Richard III a lute is "lascivious." The banished and disguised Kent tells King Lear that he is not young enough to love a woman for singing, which is to be old indeed, and some of the professional "he-men," like Hotspur and Benedick before his conversion, take up a deliberately hostile attitude toward either music or poetry. In Hotspur's case this is at least partly assumed out of his settled antagonism toward Glendower and his mixed repulsion from and attraction toward Mortimer and his Welsh wife. Hotspur is disgusted when Mortimer compares his wife's speech to

> ditties highly penn'd,
> Sung by a fair queen in a summer's bower,
> With ravishing division, to her lute,

but when the lady sings, it is clear that Hotspur wishes to hear her song, despite all his protestations to the contrary; indeed, he insists afterwards that his own wife must sing too, but that independent lady, who was quite a match for him, quite properly turns him down.[4]

Shakespeare also uses musical figures in nonmusical connections. He likes the words "consent" and "descant," and he uses harmony in music as a symbol of a higher harmony in human life. Desdemona, her husband tells us, is "an admirable musician," and it is quite suitable that Iago should resolve to "set down the pegs that make this music" between her and Othello. For this demon all life stands on its head when he looks at it, and he feels his own diabolical equivalent of the creative joy of the god or the artist

---

[4] On Shakespeare's musical background, see Fripp, pp. 124ff. and Caroline Spurgeon's analysis of his musical images, pp. 69–76. According to Marchette Chute, *Shakespeare of London* (Du, 1949), *The Comedy of Errors* is the only play which makes no use of music. Anthony Burgess, *Shakespeare* (Knopf, 1970), 252, finds that in *Love's Labour's Lost* Shakespeare composed a theme of six notes and gave it to Holofernes. "Curiously, no musician has ever taken up that theme and developed it. C D G A E F—it is suitable for a ground bass; it can be extended into a fugal subject. If we repeat it a tri-tone higher or lower, we have a perfect twelve-tone *Grundstimmung* for a serial composition. We are still waiting for Variations on a Theme by William Shakespeare."

when he manipulates the lives of others to their destruction: "Pleasure and action," he says, "make the hours seem short." Nym sums up a situation by saying "this is the very plain-song of it"; the jealous Leontes sees his wife "virginalling" on Polixenes' palm (see the interesting account of a performance on the virginals in Sonnet 128); banished Mowbray laments that with his native English no longer usable, his tongue will become "an unstringed viol or a harp"; and Hamlet of course plays a scene with Rosencrantz and Guildenstern around a recorder, the purpose of which is to convince them that they have been guilty of monstrous presumption in attempting to "play upon" him, though they admit that the simple fingering of a pipe is beyond them.

The most elaborate musical passage in Shakespeare occurs at the glorious, moon-drenched opening of the last act of *The Merchant of Venice*. Says Lorenzo:

> How sweet the moonlight sleeps upon this bank!
> Here will we sit and let the sounds of music
> Creep in our ears.

The stars are "patines of bright gold" in the floor of heaven, and this thought leads to a discussion of the music of the spheres in a highly metaphysical passage:

> There's not the smallest orb which thou behold'st
> But in his motion like an angel sings,
> Still quiring to the young-ey'd cherubins.
> Such harmony is in immortal souls;
> But whilst this muddy vesture of decay
> Doth grossly close it in, we cannot hear it.

This might be enough, but Lorenzo does not stop there. Next he describes the effect of music upon animal spirits, which in turn leads to a reference to Orpheus, and the passage closes by equating musical sensitivity with nobility of character:

> The man that hath no music in himself,
> Nor is not mov'd with concord of sweet sounds,
> Is fit for treasons, stratagems, and spoils,

The motions of his spirit are dull as night
And his affections dark as Erebus.
Let no such man be trusted.

This is indeed a cavalier equating of the good and the beautiful!
Can Shakespeare possibly have believed it? It is no doubt true that
a man who has a keen interest in any of the nobler pursuits and
interests of life may find in it a certain protection against base
temptations as well as a certain source of solace against life's trials.
But to take Lorenzo literally would be a little hard on tone-deaf
people, and though I know of no statistics in this area, I doubt it
would be easy to show that musicians and other highly musical
people are as a class either more or less moral than others. It is interesting, however, that Shakespeare causes Julius Caesar to share
Lorenzo's impression: he does not trust Cassius not only because
of his "lean and hungry look," but also because "he loves no plays"
and "hears no music." Such a test would leave Brutus' withers unwrung, for he has Lucius play to him until the boy falls asleep the
very night Caesar's ghost manifests to him before Philippi.

There was of course one other art with which Shakespeare un-
deniably had intimate personal acquaintance, and that was the art
of the theater. Players appear and take part in the action of both
Hamlet and *The Taming of the Shrew*, but Shakespeare's theatrical references are by no means confined to these plays.[5] Buckingham can "counterfeit the deep tragedian," and Richard III himself refers to the Vice of the old moralities and puts on a "scene"
for the benefit of the Lord Mayor of London when he appears on
a balcony with a bishop on either side of him. In *King John* the
citizens of Angiers

> stand securely on their battlements
> As in a theatre, whence they gape and point
> At your industrious scenes and acts of death.

Falstaff and Prince Hal enact King Henry IV and his unregenerate

---

[5] See Masson's list of references, figures, and allusions, *Shakespeare Personally*,
179ff.

son in an Eastcheap tavern, interchanging the two roles in the course of their turn. Casca compares the attitude of the mob toward Julius Caesar with that of an audience toward the players. In *The Tempest* Antony uses a theatrical figure to describe the wrecking and rescue of himself and his companions:

> We all were sea-swallow'd, though some cast again,
> And by that destiny to perform an act
> Whereof what's past is prologue, what to come
> In yours and my discharge.

Finally, in Jaques' great speech in *As You Like It* (II, 7), the world itself becomes a stage and all the men and women merely players.

In a few passages, life and the theater are daringly juxtaposed. In *Twelfth Night* Fabian declares that he could not believe in the gulling of Malvolio if he saw the scene acted upon a stage. The point of course is that he *is* seeing it acted upon a stage and the audience along with him, the latter being invited to achieve a "willing suspension of disbelief" in despite of having been specifically warned against it. Pandarus sees his name and those of the hero and heroine of *Troilus and Cressida* being used to indicate types of character long after they themselves are dead and gone, and Cleopatra does not wish to be impersonated by the "squeaking" boy actors of Rome.[6] But the most daring scene is that in *Julius Caesar*, where the conspirators bathe in Caesar's blood:

CASCA.   How many ages hence
> Shall this our lofty scene be acted over
> In states unborn and accents yet unknown!

BRUTUS.   How many times shall Caesar bleed in sport,
> That now on Pompey's basis lies along
> No worthier than the dust!

CASCA.   So oft as that shall be,

---

[6] It is sad to realize that Shakespeare never saw any of his heroines enacted by a woman. In such scenes as Rosalind's in the Forest of Arden, the Elizabethan audience had to make do with a boy pretending to be a girl who was pretending to be a boy! Either the actors must have possessed great and subtle skill or else the audience was not very particular about fine distinctions.

So often shall the knot of us be call'd
The men that gave their country liberty.

Shakespeare's discussion of the technique of the drama (as distinct from acting itself) does not get much beyond consideration of the physical limitations of the playhouse and the constricting dramatic form. Legend says that it was his recognition of the quality of *Every Man in His Humour* that gave Ben Jonson his theatrical start, but this is not certainly known. It has been suggested that he departed sharply from his usual practice to observe the unities in *The Comedy of Errors* and *The Tempest* in order to show the classicists that he could meet them on their own ground when he chose to do so, but it seems more likely that he was simply concerned to place the material which in these instances he had at his disposal in what seemed to him the most natural and effective form. But there can be no question that he is concerned with technique when, in the Prologue to *Troilus and Cressida*, he recognizes the limitations of the drama in presenting such a subject as the Trojan War; the play, we are told,

> Leaps o'er the vaunt and firstlings of these broils,
> Beginning in the middle, starting thence away
> To what may be digested in a play,

a statement which shows, further, the author's familiarity with epic theory and specifically with the advice of Horace to begin *in medias res*. Gower apologizes for the disconnectedness of *Pericles* and affirms the dramatist's right to carry the imagination of the spectator "from bourn to bourn," and if we reject this as non-Shakespearean, we shall still have the Chorus making a similar plea when bridging the gap between Acts III and IV of *The Winter's Tale*.

But it is in the choruses of *Henry V* that all these things are most fully considered, for here the dramatist is so inspired by his great theme that he craves "a kingdom for a stage" and princes for actors, instead of the "unworthy scaffold" and "cockpit" actually at his disposal, where one man must be divided into a thousand

parts and imperfections eked out by the imagination of the audience. When the scene of the action shifts from England to France, "the abuse of distance" must be "digested," and the playhouse itself transported bodily, with "the narrow seas" charmed to give the audience "gentle pass." It is interesting that Shakespeare seems to feel the limitations of the Elizabethan dramatic form more strongly when he approaches a subject which skirts the epic, rather than remaining in the strictly dramatic, mood.[7]

Ulysses was speaking for himself, not Shakespeare, when he accused Patroclus of mocking Agamemnon like "a strutting player," and Macbeth is no more out of sorts with actors than with life itself in his famous "brief candle" speech:

> Life's but a walking shadow, a poor player
> That struts and frets his hour upon the stage
> And then is heard no more.

Here again it is "struts," and one wonders whether this particular word would have been chosen by an actor very sensitive to the dignity of his profession. Shakespeare was certainly mindful of the difference between good actors and bad, as one may see by juxtaposing

> As an unperfect actor on the stage
> Who with his fear is put besides his part,

of Sonnet 23, and York's speech in *Richard II*:

> As in a theatre, the eyes of men,
> After a well-grac'd actor leaves the stage,
> Are idly bent on him that enters next,
> Thinking his prattle to be tedious;

[7] As everybody knows, Shakespeare said everything, even about matters which did not exist in his time, and I have always maintained that Theseus of *A Midsummer Night's Dream* achieved the ideal description of the "movies"—"The best in this kind are but shadows; and the worst are no worse, if imagination amend them." Both *Pericles* and *Henry V* are better adapted to screen than stage, as Laurence Olivier proved in the second instance by his famous production during World War II.

> Even so, or with much more contempt, men's eyes
> Did scowl on gentle Richard.

But there is also Sonnet 110, which, though it may not refer specifically to the actor, could hardly have been written by Shakespeare without thinking of his own profession:

> Alas, 'tis true I have gone here and there
> And made myself a motley to the view,
> Gor'd mine own thoughts, sold cheap what is most dear,
> Made old offences of affections new.[8]

The scenes involving the players in *Hamlet* are by no means wholly concerned with acting. There are topical references to the state of the London theaters in Shakespeare's time, and various types of English drama are indicated. The play presented at court, with the dumb show preceding it, involves problems and has occasioned much learned discussion which need not be summarized here except to say that its stilted, old-fashioned, highly rhetorical character seems to have been designed to set it off stylistically from the play of *Hamlet* itself. Surely the declamation recited by the First Player in Act II, Scene 2 ("This is too long," says Polonius, and for once, despite Hamlet's sharp retort, one must agree with him) would seem to testify to a taste for old-fashioned rhetoric on the part of the dramatist or at least to a confidence on his part in the ability of the audience to swallow it in pretty large doses.[9] But the best part of the Players scenes occurs at the beginning of III,

---

[8] In both the Prologue and the Epilogue to *Henry VIII* the degraded taste of the popular audience is excoriated, but I fear we cannot be sure Shakespeare is the author here. Hamlet recognizes the same phenomenon however and is well aware that the best plays are not always the most successful. Hamlet (perhaps unfairly) attributes groundling tastes to Polonius: "he's for a jig or a tale of bawdry, or he sleeps."

[9] John Semple Smart raises an interesting larger question when he declares that Shakespeare took it for granted that his audiences "were interested in poetry, and would listen, not only with toleration but with rapt interest, to the long speeches of Jaques, Hamlet, and Macbeth. He took for granted that they were attracted by allusions to classical history and classical mythology; and he took for granted that they would instantly understand phrases in Latin, French, and Italian, and would be pleased by hearing them. If Shakespeare had not made these assumptions, neither the long poetical speeches, nor the classical allusions, nor the scraps of Latin, French and Italian would ever have found a place in his works."

2, with "Speak the speech, I pray you, as I pronounc'd it to you, trippingly on the tongue." Surely more good sense about acting has never been crowded into equally narrow compass.

How good an actor was Shakespeare himself? How we should like to know! He was certainly one of the leading members of his company, but his acting was not the only ace he held. He may even have been played down as an actor in order to give him more time for writing. Tradition says that he made a very good king, but the specific roles with which his name has been more or less reliably connected, like Adam in *As You Like It* and the Ghost in *Hamlet*, do not suggest that he was ever a menace to Burbage.

II

Writing, however, especially when you are a great poet, is a larger matter than stagecraft. Shakespeare, to be sure, was not exclusively a poet. Even in the great tragedies, some important matters are dealt with in prose, and criticism has, on the whole, paid less attention to Shakespeare's prose than it deserves. Stoll noted that he uses "real" words ("the true and troubled accents of the human voice"), not searching out what is formally or conventionally beautiful.[10] Hamlet dies on "The rest is silence." "Shakespeare himself could use no more than the commonplace," says Henry Adams, "to express what is incapable of expression. . . . The few familiar words, among the simplest in the language, conveying an idea trite beyond rivalry, served Shakespeare, and, as yet, no one has said more." And Lear's amazing "Pray you, undo this button" is even plainer. None of this, however, lessens our impression of his tremendous poetic power when he chose to employ it. It does not necessarily follow, however, that he entertained an elaborate literary theory. "Style? I never think of style," cried the in some ways Shakespearean Sir Walter Scott. "I have had regiments of cavalry marching through my head since I was fourteen." Shakespeare might have spared the cavalry, but it does not follow that we are likely to catch him talking about his "art."

[10] Elmer Edgar Stoll, *Shakespeare Studies* (M, 1927), 34.

After his early poems, he seems to have devoted himself wholly to writing for the stage, apparently making no effort to publish or to preserve what he produced. Did he lack ambition? was he just too busy as a practical theater man to write anything but plays?[11] or was he a keen enough self-critic to realize that it was in the popular drama that his real strength lay? Certainly he produced a tremendous amount of work in a not overlong theatrical career which embraced other activities besides playwriting; he must have worked steadily and hard. The length of some of his plays suggests, too, that he sometimes wrote more than could be performed, so that his text had to be cut in production, which does not look like a writer who was writing for bread alone or one performing a stipulated task in a mechanical manner or incapable of being carried away by his inspiration.

He was, of course, an extremely careless writer, as careless indeed as even one of his transcendent genius could afford to be. Lowell's "bardolatry" was never more ill-advised than when he proposed to adhere to the Folio as authority "in all cases where it does not make Shakespeare write bad sense, uncouth metre, or false grammar, of all which I believe him to have been more supremely incapable than any other man who ever wrote English."[12] The truth is that Shakespeare was as richly entitled to these privileges as anybody else, and surely no other writer ever more joyously availed himself of them.[13] He could do anything with the English language that any writer has ever done, but he also inflicted upon it every cruelty and indignity it can be made to suffer. And he grew worse, not better, in this matter, as he grew older.

Anachronisms are so common—and well recognized—in Shakespeare that only a few examples need be given. Gloucester uses spectacles in Lear's Britain, Thaliard has a pistol in *Pericles*, and

11 "Pete the parrot and shakespeare," Section XXVIII of Don Marquis' *archy and mehitabel* (D, 1930) is a hilarious fantasy on the subject of "poor Bill's" indifference to his plays and frustrated desire to be a poet!
12 "Shakespeare Once More," in *Among My Books*.
13 See Alfred Harbage, "The Myth of Perfection," in *Conceptions of Shakespeare* (HUP, 1966).

there are Elizabethan rushes on the floor in *Cymbeline*. A clock strikes in Caesar's Rome, and knighthood is an established institution in *Titus Andronicus*. And if the proper Victorian lady who was shocked by a performance of *Antony and Cleopatra* had paid more attention to Cleopatra's asking Charmian to cut her lace, she might even have felt that there was less difference than she had supposed between what went on in the palace at Alexandria and "the home life of our dear Queen."

These things did not go wholly unnoted even in Shakespeare's own time. Ben Jonson went after his friend for giving Bohemia a seacoast and boasted that he himself was "loath to make nature afraid in his plays, like those that beget tales, tempests, and such-like drolleries." If the editors of the First Folio boasted of Shakespeare that "his mind and hand went together," so that he uttered what he thought with such easiness "that we have scarce received from him a blot in his papers," the classical perfectionist Jonson could reply, "Would he had blotted a thousand."

Shakespeare was careless with both his sources and his own inventions. In *As You Like It* Rosalind is both taller than Celia and shorter; first one Duke is called Frederick, then the other; there are inconsistent statements concerning the length of time the banished Duke has lived in Arden. In *The Winter's Tale* he followed his source to combine Delos, the island where Apollo was born, with Delphi, where the oracle sat, and came up with Delphos. And in *Antony and Cleopatra* (IV, 12) we are told that swallows have built their nests in Cleopatra's sails and that this was regarded as an evil omen. What Plutarch says is that "swallows had bred under the poop of her ship and there came others after them that drave away the first and plucked down their nests." This was the evil omen. But the summary in the margin of North's translation is misleading: "An ill sign, foreshadowed by swallows breeding in Cleopatra's ship," and Shakespeare evidently read the margin and did not bother with the text! Here, for one fleeting moment, we catch a fascinating glimpse of the dramatist at work on one of his plays.

Compared to some of his fellows, Shakespeare would not seem

to have been much given to topical references. "I do not my
believe," wrote Sir Edmund K. Chambers, "that, apart from so
passages of obvious satire in comic scenes, there is much of the
topical in Shakespeare, whose mind normally moved upon quite
another plane of relation to life."[14] So it would indeed seem with
a dramatist who ostensibly set only one of his least significant
plays—The Merry Wives of Windsor—in his contemporary England, but of course foreign materials have often been given an
Elizabethan coloring, and there may be many true topical references in the plays which we do not understand. Love's Labour's
Lost is steeped in every fashionable interest of the Renaissance;
the life of a great Elizabethan household seems mirrored in
Twelfth Night;[15] and the tavern activities described in the Henry
IV plays are certainly not distinctively fifteenth century.

[14] William Shakespeare: A Survey of Facts and Problems (OUP), II, 67.
[15] See John W. Draper, "Olivia's Household," PMLA, XLIX (1934), 797–
806. Many source hunters have been seduced into far more doubtful paths than
any I have so far explored, notably Lilian Winstanley in an extremely wild but
immensely entertaining series of books: Hamlet and the Scottish Succession; Macbeth, King Lear and Contemporary History; Othello and the Tragedy of Italy
(CUP, 1921, 1922, 1924). Since Miss Winstanley had the gift of making anything
represent whatever it suited her protean theories to have it represent at the moment,
her views are impossible to summarize, but no lover of detective stories could possibly fail to enjoy her books, though not, I fear, in quite the way she could have
wished them to be enjoyed. For her Hamlet was both James I and the Earl of
Essex, and Shakespeare wrote his play around the two subjects which at the time
of writing most occupied his mind—the Scottish succession and the fate of the
Essex conspirators. Gertrude was Mary Queen of Scots and Polonius Lord Burleigh.
Othello became an allegory of the domination of Italy by Spain, with Othello as
Philip II and Iago as Antonio Perez. The Darnley tragedy was used again in King
Lear, but this time Miss Winstanley crossed it with the murder of Admiral Coligny
and the Massacre of St. Bartholomew. Lear was both Darnley and Coligny, and
Goneril and Regan were both Mary Queen of Scots—except when Regan was
somebody else.
    Poor stupid Essex has apparently exercised an irresistible fascination for those
hungry to trace out historical allegories. Dixon Wecter, "The Purpose of Timon
of Athens," PMLA, XLIII (1928), 701–21, thought that play concerned with
his fall, and Evelyn May Albright's "Shakespeare's Richard II and the Essex Conspiracy," PMLA, XLII (1927), 686–720 involved her in prolonged and sometimes
bitter controversy with Ray Heffner. But all this was surpassed (probably everything was surpassed) by James Westfall Thompson, "Hamlet and Amy Robsart,"
North American Review, CCXV (1922), 657–72, where the murder of the elder
Hamlet became the death of Amy Robsart! This would make Claudius Leicester
and Gertrude Queen Elizabeth. Who Hamlet was Thompson did not stop to
inquire.

A considerable number of supposed topical references in Shakespeare have been pointed out from time to time; some of these still seem fairly safe while many more have now been given up because the event in question was too early or too late or because the alleged resemblance is not close enough to be convincing. It still seems reasonable to suppose that the "fair vestal throned by the west" who escaped Cupid's shaft and "passed on/ In maiden meditation fancy free" was meant for Queen Elizabeth and that *Macbeth* was written with an eye to the interests of King James I. The Earl of Essex was all but named in the Prologue to the last act of *Henry V*, which was first produced when he was about to return from the great military adventure which ironically led to his destruction:

> Were now the general of our gracious empress,
> As in good time he may, from Ireland coming,
> Bringing rebellion broached on his sword,
> How many would the peaceful city quit,
> To welcome him!

The War of the Theaters is certainly considered in *Hamlet*, and it

---

One other article ought to be mentioned in this connection, and this was the work of the great Chaucer scholar, Edith Rickert, "Political Propaganda and Satire in *A Midsummer Night's Dream*," *Modern Philology*, XXXI (1923), 53–87, 133–54. Miss Rickert regarded the play as propaganda in behalf of the Earl of Hertford, who, according to the will of Henry VIII, was next in succession to the throne after Elizabeth. Elizabeth is Titania, and Oberon, whose will she crosses, is Henry VIII. Bottom is King James VI of Scotland, who was to become King James I of England. All this was argued with great skill and learning, but few appear to have been convinced.

We have often been told that there is only a limited number of basic plots which may be used in fiction; no doubt it is also true that only a limited number of basic situations can exist in life. Perhaps this is the reason why so many mutually exclusive interpretations of the same situation can be worked out by sufficiently ingenious commentators. Even I could find Mary Queen of Scots in Shakespeare if I really set out to do so. "It is yours," says Paulina to Leontes of the new-born Perdita,

And might we lay th' old proverb to your charge,
So like you, 'tis the worse.

Mary said something very like this to Darnley after the birth of James. And Cleopatra's questions about Octavia in *Antony and Cleopatra* (III, 3) strongly suggest Elizabeth's jealous inquiries about Mary herself.

is still generally believed that the "new map with the augmentation of the Indies" in *Twelfth Night* was a particular map published in 1599. Malvolio, interfering with Sir Toby's roistering, may or may not be Sir Andrew Willoughby, Queen Elizabeth's Chief Sewer and Squire of the Presence breaking up a game of primero between Southampton and Raleigh in the presence chamber after her Majesty had retired, as Sir Israel Gollancz believed, or he may be Sir William Knollys, Comptroller of the Royal Household, who objected to being disturbed by the "frisking" and "heying" of some of the maids of honor, as Sir Edmund Chambers suggested. The great "bed of Ware," also spoken of in *Twelfth Night*, was—and is—a real bed. The "Witch of Brainford" (= Brentford) in *The Merry Wives* was an actual tavern keeper in that place, and "Marian Hacket, the fat ale-wife of Wincot," mentioned in *The Taming of the Shrew* by Christopher Sly, "old Sly's son of Burton heath," where Shakespeare's aunt lived, was in all probability a well-known local character also. The eccentric German count, Frederick of Mömpelgart, who made himself a considerable nuisance to Queen Elizabeth, is apparently referred to in *The Merry Wives*, and the same play contains court allusions and references to Windsor which would certainly have more point if the play were acted before the Queen, as tradition alleges. On the other hand, the long-credited references to Sir Thomas Lucy now seem rather worse than doubtful,[16] nor are we

---

[16] Leslie Hotson, *Shakespeare vs. Shallow* (Little Brown, 1931) made a case for the thesis that Shallow is a caricature of William Gardiner, a notorious—and disgustingly wealthy—public official of Shakespeare's time, and that Slender is his nephew, William Wayte. Gardiner's first wife was a Lucy, and by his marriage he gained the right to use the Lucy coat of arms, which he exercised. Shallow's attempt to marry Slender to Anne Page was, as Hotson sees it, a hit at Gardiner's marrying Wayte to a young heiress named Joan Tayler. We know that Shakespeare and an Elizabethan theatrical manager named Francis Langley had serious difficulties with Gardiner, and that at one time Wayte had them put under peace bonds, alleging that they had threatened his life.

Sir Herbert Beerbohm Tree's productions of *Henry VIII* and *The Merry Wives of Windsor* were the most gorgeous stage spectacles I have ever seen, and when Sir Herbert presented them in Chicago late in 1916, he made the cleverest curtain speech I have ever heard. *The Merry Wives*, he reminded us, was supposed to have been written at the request of Queen Elizabeth, who wished to see Falstaff in love. "You may be sure," he added, "that the play was to Queen Elizabeth's taste," which drew the laugh he had expected. Then, turning the joke upon the audience,

by any means so sure as we once were that the "coal of fire upon the ice" in *Coriolanus* refers to the freezing over of the Thames in 1608 nor that any particular period in French history is referred to in the description of that country in *The Comedy of Errors* as "armed and reverted, making war against her heir." And though in a sense the winds which wafted the New World explorers do blow through *The Tempest*, where Ariel fetches dew at midnight "from the still-vex'd Bermoothes," there are no specific references.

There are times, one must admit, when even Shakespeare's inconsistencies, anachronisms, and presumed carelessness evidence the boldness of genius. In *The Merchant of Venice* the bond story needs three months while the love story cannot possibly use more than three days. But it suits the design of the play to have the news that Shylock has foreclosed reach Bassanio in the very moment he has won Portia. This, accordingly, is what happens. The intensity and condensation of the drama are immensely strengthened, and it seems safe to say that nobody has ever been troubled by the discrepancy while watching a performance. Similarly, in *Othello* you can prove from the text both that Desdemona is murdered within little more than twenty-four hours after her arrival in Cyprus (her marriage not having been consummated in Venice) and that she and Othello have been living together in happy, settled, peaceful wedlock for some little time. Evidently Shakespeare desired the force which the tragedy gains from being developed at breakneck speed, but he also wished to create the impression that a situation of settled peace and harmony had been destroyed by Iago's machinations. So he again combines the two effects, to the discomfiture of pedants (in whom he had no interest) but to the profit of the ordinary theater-goer (for whom he wrote). He cannot possibly have been so stupid as to do these things without knowing what he was doing, though I am very ready to believe that he did not consider any of it important enough to be steadily and consciously held in his mind.

---

he added, "I am glad it was also to your taste," and, after a pause just long enough to permit the situation to be savored, he removed the sting by concluding, "That shows what good taste Queen Elizabeth had."

As to Shakespeare's attitude toward poetry itself, modern readers of the Sonnets are sometimes inclined to find the oft-repeated promises of immortality through verse not only proud but arrogant.

> Not marble nor the gilded monuments
> Of princes shall outlive this pow'rful rhyme;
> But you shall shine more bright in these contents
> Than unswept stone besmear'd with sluttish time.

The arrogance, however, if that be the word, is largely conventional; even in the Sonnets there are references to "my slight muse," "my barren rhyme," and "these poor rude lines," and there are two poems (76 and 105) in which the poet complains of the monotony of his themes and treatment, a complaint which many students of Elizabethan sonneteering have echoed. In the plays what is said about poetry seems rather sparse and slighting. Touchstone equates it with feigning and finds no honesty in it. The poet in *Timon of Athens* is a sycophant and a fool, and in *Julius Caesar* Cinna is lynched by the mob which Antony's eloquence has fired because he bears the same name as one of the conspirators. It does him no good to protest that he is Cinna the poet, not Cinna the conspirator; they are glad to have somebody to lynch on any terms, and if they cannot hang him for conspiracy, they will hang him for his bad verses. Brutus does not employ violence when the poet rebukes him for his quarrel with Cassius, but he can hardly be called very respectful: "What should the wars do with these juggling fools?"

The most important passage by far is given to Theseus in *A Midsummer Night's Dream*:

> The lunatic, the lover, and the poet
> Are of imagination all compact.
> One sees more devils than vast hell can hold;
> That is, the madman. The lover, all as frantic,
> Sees Helen's beauty in a brow of Egypt.
> The poet's eye, in a fine frenzy rolling,

51

Doth glance from heaven to earth, from earth to heaven;
And as imagination bodies forth
The forms of things unknown, the poet's pen
Turns them to shapes and gives to airy nothing
A local habitation and a name.

Though poetry is here somewhat disrespectfully associated with madness, all readers must feel that Shakespeare does show his understanding of the creative process.

It may well be that in Theseus Shakespeare is saying that a good ruler must have sensitiveness and imagination, but he surely knew that poetry and moral idealism do not always go together. For one of his most morally worthless characters is steeped in both poetry and humor (a difficult combination!); this, of course, is Sir John Falstaff. To Falstaff thieves are "squires of the night's body," men of "good government" because they are governed by their "noble and chaste mistress the moon," under whose countenance they steal. The white-bearded old scoundrel takes it upon himself to assert the claims of youth against crabbed age (measuring "the heat of our livers with the bitterness of your galls"), and he laments with true, pious indignation the inability of rascals to be true to one another. Even Bardolph's sack-inflamed "salamander" nose fires his imagination; has it not saved him a thousand marks in links and torches while finding his way from tavern to tavern after nightfall? And though the Chief Justice is quite right when he finds Falstaff using his imagination for the purpose of "wrenching the true cause the false way," there is no denying the imagination itself. Falstaff does not deny his frailty, but since flesh *is* frail, and he has much more of it than other men, he thinks he should be excused for his frailties. Shakespeare's instinct did not play him false when he brought Falstaff into a mock fairy scene in the forest at the end of *The Merry Wives of Windsor*, nor did Verdi's when he went considerably further and composed some of the most magical music in all opera for this scene. Perhaps Falstaff "babbled of green fields" when he lay dying only in Theobald's imagination, but if so, then for once an editor dis-

played an imagination worthy of Shakespeare himself.[17] The fat knight's frequent references to Scripture are profane, not pious, evidencing the "strain of the perverted Puritan" in him. But the point is that he is not a pagan but a lapsed Christian. Once upon a time, the Bible did mean something to him, and to his higher, more imaginative self it does still. He can scuttle it and soil it and trample upon it, but he cannot forget it, and its stylistic glories still echo through his brain. Moreover, though it has been many years now since he had any interest in any human being except for what he could get out of him, his insight into character has not yet wholly deserted him. In 2 *Henry IV* (IV, 3), when he has nearly run his course, he plays a descant on the differences between Prince Hal and his brother, Prince John of Lancaster. We must not permit the fact that he arbitrarily and absurdly proceeds to associate these differences with the fact that Hal drinks wine and John does not, to blind us to the fact that he is right about the contrast, for John promptly justifies him by his treacherous betrayal of the rebels who have surrendered to him.

III

Bernard Shaw, who nearly always talked wisely about Shakespeare except when he was unable to get his mind off himself long enough to fix it upon his subject, was quite right to attribute his greatness as a writer to the grandeur of his style, "his enormous command of word-music," rather than to his prowess as an independent thinker, and Elmer Edgar Stoll was right also when he saw him creating character not by reference to the processes of psychological analysis which many modern novelists favor but rather by creating speech rhythms illustrative of individual character. In such a discussion as we have here in hand, the beauty and power of Shakespeare's style are illustrated in almost everything one finds it necessary to quote from him for any purpose; here, for a moment, let us turn our attention to style for its own sake. I will say nothing of the great "set" pieces—arias one might call them in

[17] The Folio reads "and a Table of greene fields." Theobald took the dying man's mind back to the Twenty-third Psalm.

53

operatic terms—Portia's mercy speech, Mercutio's Queen Mab speech, the Seven Ages of Man in *As You Like It*, Antony's oration, the description of Cleopatra's barge, Hamlet's soliloquies, and the rest of them.[18] Nor am I most interested in the conventionally "beautiful" lyrical passages, like Viola's willow cabin speech in *Twelfth Night* (I, 5); Hamlet's

> But, look, the morn, in russet mantle clad,
> Walks o'er the dew of yon high eastern hill;

or Romeo's

> Look, love, what envious streaks
> Do lace the severing clouds in yonder east.
> Night's candles are burnt out, and jocund day
> Stands tiptoe on the misty mountain tops.

Let us look first at some of the briefer sententious utterances:

> Nor I nor any man that but man is,
> With nothing shall be pleas'd, till he be eas'd
> With being nothing.
> > *Richard II*

> Uneasy lies the head that wears a crown.
> > *2 Henry IV*

> There is some soul of goodness in things evil,
> Would men observingly distil it out.
> > *Henry V*

> The fault, dear Brutus, is not in our stars,
> But in ourselves, that we are underlings.
> > *Julius Caesar*

---

[18] It may be noted here that though there is some "difficult" writing in Shakespeare, especially in the later plays, none of these lines, not even the famous cruces, give any trouble when they are spoken rapidly in the theater. *Antony and Cleopatra* (III, 1:16–17):

> Ho! hearts, tongues, figures, scribes, bards, poets cannot
> Think, speak, cast, write, sing, number, ho!

is a respective construction with no fewer than six pairs of words contained in it, but what listener was ever troubled by it?

Cowards die many times before their deaths;
The valiant never taste of death but once.
Julius Caesar

There is a tide in the affairs of men
Which, taken at the flood, leads on to fortune;
Omitted, all the voyage of their life
Is bound in shallows and in miseries.
Julius Caesar

One touch of nature makes the whole world kin.
Troilus and Cressida

There are more things in heaven and earth, Horatio,
Than are dreamt of in our philosophy.
Hamlet

There is nothing either good or bad but thinking makes it so.
Hamlet

There's a divinity that shapes our ends,
Rough-hew them how we will.
Hamlet

Speak of me as I am; nothing extenuate,
Nor aught set down in malice.
Othello

Men must endure
Their going hence even as their coming hither;
Ripeness is all.
King Lear

More is thy due than more than all can pay.
Macbeth

Who is't can read a woman?
Cymbeline

Hamlet and *Julius Caesar* are particularly rich in this kind of thing.
Sometimes Shakespeare builds comparisons or achieves analogies which (one is tempted to say) could have occurred to no one else:

55

I go alone/ Like to a lonely dragon.

Coriolanus

Lilies that fester smell far worse than weeds.

Sonnet 94

If I be serv'd such another trick, I'll have my brains ta'en out and butter'd, and give them to a dog for a new-year's gift.

The Merry Wives of Windsor

I tell you, my lord fool, out of this nettle, danger, we pluck this flower, safety.[19]

1 Henry IV

Sometimes an ordinary thought becomes memorable because it is expressed in an extraordinary way:

I count myself in nothing else so happy
As in a soul rememb'ring my good friends.

Richard II

The hand that made you fair hath made you good.

Measure for Measure

Let us not burden our remembrances with
A heaviness that's gone.

The Tempest

And sometimes even nonsense is unforgettable:

I did impeticos thy gratility.[20]

Twelfth Night

---

[19] Katherine Mansfield was so moved by this that she used it as an epigraph on one of her books; later it seemed so characteristic of her life and of her spirit that it was engraved upon her tombstone.

[20] Nothing was ever better done in kind than much of Mistress Quickly's senseless blabbering, especially the long speech in her quarrel with Falstaff in *2 Henry IV* (II, 1:92ff.) If the reader does not fully savor this upon the printed page, let him listen to Dame Edith Evans' reading of it in the Caedmon recording of the play. I confess that until I heard this recording, I had no idea how amusing Mistress Quickly's tiresome objections to "swaggering" could be made. The Caedmon recording of *Romeo and Juliet* bears further testimony to the skill of this artist. If Shakespeare had never done anything better than the lines he gave the Nurse in the scene where Juliet is found, supposedly dead, on her wedding morn, we can hardly suppose he would enjoy a very great reputation. But as Dame Edith does this scene, nobody is going to be bored by it.

Finally, under this head, there are passages which carry suggestions beyond their context, sometimes no doubt even beyond
Shakespeare's intention. In 1 *Henry IV* Douglas declares, "We
may boldly spend upon the hope of what/ Is to come in." Where
is there a better statement of the whole principle of modern in-
stallment buying? Having accepted bribes from able-bodied men
who can pay to escape military service, Falstaff cries, "Will you
tell me, Master Shallow, how to choose a man? Care I for the
limb, the thews, the stature, bulk, and big assemblance of a man!
Give me the spirit, Master Shallow." Polonius counsels Laertes:

> This above all: to thine own self be true,
> And it must follow, as the night the day,
> Thou canst not then be false to any man.

Falstaff is merely covering up his own cupidity and hypocrisy, and
Polonius being what he is, his advice amounts merely to "Look out
for Number One." Yet in both cases (and in Falstaff's too) the
words uttered are also susceptible of a higher meaning which is far
more noble, and when they are quoted out of context, such sense
is often imputed to them. More interesting still is Macbeth's

> Let every man be master of his time
> Till seven at night.

"Master of his time"—what a noble phrase! Time is the stuff of
life; to master one's time is to be master of one's life. But all Macbeth means is that his guests are to have what travel agents call a
"free period." Until dinner time nothing is "programmed," and
every man may do as he likes. Apparently Shakespeare could not
say even commonplace things in a commonplace manner, yet he
miraculously avoids overweighting unimportant speeches and
scenes, and so his plays are not thrown off balance, as they sometimes are in performance when an actor of great fame or genius is
cast in a minor role.

In the last analysis, however, what impresses me most in connection with Shakespeare's use of language is his overwhelming
array of brief, suggestive, imagination-tingling phrases (many of

57

them not even complete sentences); titles and epigraphs without number have been drawn from such phrases, and some of them have even passed into common speech. Only a few examples out of many can be given here, but perhaps these will serve to give the flavor:

> Ports and happy havens.
>> *Richard II*

> The virtue of this jest.
>> *1 Henry IV*

> Redeeming time when men least think I will.
>> *1 Henry IV*

> Time . . . must have a stop.
>> *1 Henry IV*

> We have heard the chimes at midnight.
>> *2 Henry IV*

> Familiar in his mouth as household words.
>> *Henry V*

> There's pippins and cheese to come.
>> *The Merry Wives of Windsor*

> At the latter end of a sea-coal fire.
>> *The Merry Wives of Windsor*

> The world's mine oyster.
>> *The Merry Wives of Windsor*

> Matter for a May morning.
>> *Twelfth Night*

> Thus the whirligig of time brings in his revenges.
>> *Twelfth Night*

> Season your admiration for a while.
>> *Hamlet*

> A countenance more/In sorrow than in anger.
>> *Hamlet*

> The glimpses of the moon.
>> *Hamlet*

Caviare to the general.

Hamlet

The rest is silence.

Hamlet

You are one of those that will not serve
God if the devil bid you.

Othello

One that loved not wisely but too well.

Othello

We are not the first/Who with best meaning have incurr'd
the worst.

King Lear

I'll make assurance double sure/And take a bond of fate.

Macbeth

My salad days/When I was green in judgment.

Antony and Cleopatra

He will to his Egyptian dish again.

Antony and Cleopatra

Cleopatra hath nodded him to her.

Antony and Cleopatra

I found you as a morsel cold upon
Dead Caesar's trencher.

Antony and Cleopatra

The world's great snare.

Antony and Cleopatra

Darkling stand/The varying shore o' the world.

Antony and Cleopatra

The print of his remembrance

Cymbeline

A snapper-up of unconsidered trifles.

The Winter's Tale

Unpath'd waters, undream'd shores.

The Winter's Tale

But O, the thorns we stand upon!

The Winter's Tale

IV

MEN AND WOMEN

I

Shakespeare could write, then. But "you can't write writing." What did he write about? and what did he have to say?

He wrote about men and women in this world, and his attitude toward them was kindly. "Shakespeare," said Kittredge, "is the great assertor of the ineradicable soundness of human nature." And though terrible things sometimes happen in his plays, surely every sensitive reader must feel without argument that his general tone is humane and comparatively gentle.[1] Villains like Oliver and

[1] Alfred Harbage, *As They Liked It* (M, 1947) finds that among 775 Shakespeare characters, 49 per cent are "indubitably good," 20 per cent good in the main, 14 per cent bad in the main, and only 17 per cent indubitably bad. The only plays in which the bad characters outnumber the good are *Troilus and Cressida* and *Timon of Athens*. In the plays as a whole, 69 per cent are on the side of right— 68 per cent of the men and 74 per cent of the women. In the comedies the proportion of good people runs as high as 96 per cent. Bad women are rare in comedy. "But in tragedy the bad women outnumber the good. . . . For Shakespeare it meant woe to the world when the women went wrong." Social status did not cause much variation in these percentages: the figure for good upper-class characters was 68 per cent, for the middle-class 72 per cent, and for the lower class 67 per cent. Harbage finds that Shakespeare differs on this point from other dramatists of his time and even from Spenser: "it is . . . a rare forester or fisherman in *The Faerie Queene*, who does not attempt rape or robbery." He finds further that when Shakespeare alters a character taken from one of his sources, he generally elevates him: "cer-

Duke Frederick in *As You Like It,* Iachimo in *Cymbeline,* and (in part) Edmund in *King Lear,* repent and are forgiven. Not being a sentimentalist, Shakespeare knew that this was impossible for creatures like Goneril and Regan, Iago, and Aaron.[2] It would not

tainly no pure woman in the sources becomes an impure woman in the plays." Miss Spurgeon was also impressed by Shakespeare's tenderness toward beggars and other humble people. This is one of the many aspects in which he resembled Scott, though he did not, like Scott, use such people as leading characters. A. L. Rowse, *Shakespeare, A Biography* (Harper and Row, 1963), notes that even in the maunderings of silly old Shallow and his cronies, there is "the pathos of old men remembering, or misremembering, their youth as the days close in upon them."

[2] Aaron is humanized in a measure by his love for his child, but this is minimized by his determination to bring him up to be as wicked as himself. His speech in Act V, Scene 2 (ll. 124-44) is so fantastic an avowal of his devotion to evil as to be almost comic to modern audiences. Outside of *Titus Andronicus* (if it be his), Shakespeare did not often go in for what later came to be called "Gothick" horrors, but when he needed a sinister atmosphere, with or without an admixture of supernaturalism, he had no more difficulty in conjuring it up than Hawthorne, Walter de la Mare, Marjorie Bowen, or any other modern master was to have after him. Richard III is (probably unhistorically) a deformed Gothic monster, and Richard II characteristically mingles horror with his all-pervading sentimentalism:

> For God's sake let us sit upon the ground,
> And tell sad stories of the death of kings,

which is about as good an example of what has been called blowing out the gas to see how dark it is as may be found in literature. Juliet indulges in morbid imaginings about what she would be willing to undergo to escape Paris and again later, when she pictures the terrors of the tomb in her potion speech. Imogen has a horrible scene with the headless body of Cloten, which she is supposed to mistake for that of her husband, Posthumus, and the praise Constance (*King John*) offers to "amiable lovely death" seems all the more disgusting when placed beside Sir Walter Raleigh's noble apostrophe. But Macbeth is the character who is really devoted to horror above any other in Shakespeare. Planning Banquo's murder, he prays,

> Come, seeling night,
> Scarf up the tender eye of pitiful day,
> And with thy bloody and invisible hand
> Cancel and tear to pieces that great bond
> Which keeps me pale! Light thickens, and the crow
> Makes wing to th' rooky wood;
> Good things of day begin to droop and drowse,
> Whiles night's black agents to their preys do rouse.

It would hardly be an exaggeration to say that as Romeo and Juliet have glorified young love, Macbeth has spoiled night, and at this point he has quite outrun his wife in evil, for she cannot endure the darkness but "has light by her continually." But Macbeth himself is more interesting in this connection as he goes to murder Duncan.

> Thou [sure] and firm set earth
> Hear not my steps, which [way they] walk, for fear

have been emotionally satisfying to have Iago and Aaron escape punishment, but the dramatist wisely postpones their punishment beyond the confines of the play. The unspeakable Cloten of *Cymbeline* is blotted out but not by deliberate vengeance. The Macbeths, who are not wholly bad, pay for their sins with their lives, he in battle, she by suicide in despair. Cymbeline's queen, who is almost as fantastic an image of evil as Cloten himself, also dies in despair, but much less convincingly.[3]

There are exceptions to all this. The sharp tone of *Love's Labour's Lost* is not endearing, and one understands why Hazlitt felt that if we had to give up one of Shakespeare's plays, this would be the one to relinquish. But the principal exception to everything I have been saying would seem to be Parolles in *All's Well That Ends Well*. If he is not the worst character in Shakespeare, he may well be the most disgusting, but though one cannot say that he does not deserve the punishment meted out to him, one may still gag at the calculated vulgarity with which it is administered. The enemies of Parolles are too much absorbed by the evil they combat; they are monopolized by their interest in it to such an extent that, for the time being, nothing else seems to have any meaning for them. One accepts what they do to him, but one may well shudder at what they are doing to themselves.

This seems all the more striking when *All's Well* is placed be-

---

of what?—of detection? no!—rather, for fear

> The very stones prate of my whereabout
> And take the present horror from the time,
> Which now suits with it.

The present "atmosphere" is just right; he would not change it. For what he has to do he needs all the horror he can get; he would like to get drunk on horror. Macbeth enjoys feeling "creepy." See Albert H. Tolman, "Studies in Macbeth," *The Views about Hamlet and Other Essays* (HM, 1904).

[3] Falstaff, as always, is a special case. Though such critics as Bradley and Quiller-Couch have found it impossible to accept Hal's rejection of him, nobody questions that Shakespeare intended us to accept it and that he has prepared carefully for it. "The king hath run bad humours on the knight," says Nym, and Quickly's wonderful account of his death glorifies both him and the brainless wonder who utters it. Perhaps the dramatist is not quite free of the accusation of sentimentality here, for we have seen nothing in the knight to indicate any capacity for deep feeling. But doubtless Shakespeare knew as well as we do that a bad man may have charm and that a good one may, most unfortunately, lack it altogether.

side what is in a sense its companion play, *Measure for Measure*. Lucio may or may not be quite as bad as Parolles, but one can hardly pretend that it would gratify the old Adam less to take him out and step on him. Mercy is shown him nevertheless, and, for all the rhetorical exaggeration of his "Marrying a punk, my lord, is pressing to death, whipping, and hanging," he is handled with no such sadism as has appeared in *All's Well*. Angelo, who is guilty of far greater wrong, is pardoned also, and even the "desperately mortal" Barnardine, who had left himself without any function in the drama when he refused to fulfill the purpose for which he had been created, that of dying in Claudio's stead, is kindly re-membered at the end only in order to be presented with a wholly undeserved pardon.

The Elizabethan drama in general is aristocratic in the sense that the serious characters are nearly all persons of rank and social position, and a variety of critics from Tolstoy on down have called Shakespeare antidemocratic. Not much can be said for the mobs in either *Julius Caesar* or *Coriolanus*. The common folk in the tavern scenes of *Henry IV* inspire no great respect, and the local color innyard scene shows the carriers in league with thieves. But the snapshots of the commonalty in *King John* (IV, 2:186–202) are not unsympathetic, and though Richard II's Queen finds the gardener in Act III, Scene 4 a "little better thing than earth," Shakespeare allows him to talk more sensibly than her husband ever does. The citizens in *Richard III* (II, 3) are sensible enough also, and in Act III, Scene 7 they are perspicacious and brave. In the *Henry VI* plays the uprising of 1450 is degraded from a justi-fiable protest against intolerable abuses to buffoonery, but though Jack Cade is monstrously ignorant, crying for the moon and kick-ing against the pricks of life (like all demagogues, making prom-ises that could not possibly be fulfilled), even he is given a moment of sincere human feeling at the end. In *The Merry Wives of Windsor* two women of the middle-class gull a recreant knight; they respect their own chastity, and we gain the impression that Shakespeare respected it also and took it for granted that the audience would do so as well. Savages he glanced at only in *The*

63

Tempest, where Caliban is less degraded than the dregs of civilization with whom he is temporarily allied, and more hope is held out for him.

If Shakespeare was repelled by the lower-classes, I do not think it frivolous to suggest that the basic reason was purely physical: they did not smell good! The foul-smelling breath of the Roman mob is prominent in both *Julius Caesar* and *Coriolanus.* Hamlet is repelled by the odor of Yorick's skull, and Bottom urges the mechanicals to eat no garlic before appearing in the play; on the other hand, Imogen's breath is so sweet that it perfumes the chamber where she lies. One wonders how so sensitive a man ever managed to last out his time in the London theaters of his day. On the other hand, the Amazonian heroine of *Venus and Adonis* sweats copiously in her heat, and when she swoons Adonis "wrings her nose" to help bring her to, both touches worthy to stand with Spenser's reference to Una's "fair blubbered face" in *The Faerie Queene.* And what are we to make of the Epilogue to *As You Like It,* where Rosalind not only anticipates all the oral hygiene advertisements by speaking of bad breath as an obstacle to kissing but also remarks casually that "very good orators, when they are out, they will spit"! Verily, other times, other manners.

There are a number of more serious passages, however, which seem to reflect Shakespeare's faith in the common decency of humanity. The cynical heartlessness of the musicians after Juliet's supposed death at the end of Act IV is repellent, but it is also exceptional. In *The Winter's Tale* both the Clown and the Shepherd his father show real humanity. The second murderer of Clarence in *Richard III* repents, and both Dighton and Forrest lament the killing of the princes in the Tower, though they do not prevent it. Hubert finally does his best to save Arthur, though he afterward tries to make himself out more innocent than he really was. The loyalty of Flavius to Timon of Athens is about the only ray of light in the play in which he appears.

The two most remarkable passages, however, are in *Othello* and *King Lear.* In Act IV, Scene 1 of *Othello* Shakespeare goes to some length to draw the character contrast between Desdemona's

idealism and Emilia's coarse practicality. The woman whom her husband has branded whore and treated like the inmate of a brothel can hardly conceive what he means; she actually finds it difficult to believe that there are women in the world who "do abuse their husbands." Emilia, on the other hand, has no illusions about men.

> They are all but stomachs, and we all but food;
> They eat us hungrily, and when they are full
> They belch us.

But she has no illusions about women either, nor about herself. No slave of passion, she

> would not do such a thing for a joint-ring, nor for measures of lawn, nor for gowns, petticoats, nor caps, nor any pretty exhibition; but for the whole world,—(ud's pity), who would not make her husband a cuckold to make him a monarch? I should venture purgatory for't.

And this is the woman who, when Desdemona is murdered, forgets everything else in her loyalty to her wronged mistress, and who, when at last she understands the part her husband has played in this outrage, risks and then spends her life for truth and honor. Iago's utter amazement ("What, are you mad? I charge you, get you home") is one of the subtlest touches in the play. He is honestly indignant. Like Dante's damned souls in hell, he has "lost the good of the understanding"; he has forgotten, if he ever knew, how even half-decent people react to monstrous outrage. Through Emilia's common throat, the voice of humanity speaks; she dies in her finest hour, and we forget all her faults.

The passage in *Lear* is even more remarkable. It occurs in connection with the blinding of Gloucester in Act III, Scene 7, the most sadistic scene in Shakespeare, at least outside *Titus Andronicus*. Shakespeare did not even bother to give the "First Servant" a name, but he did have him cry out:

> Hold your hand, my lord!
> I have serv'd you ever since I was a child;

But better service have I never done you
Than now to bid you hold.

Nor does he stop with that, but takes a sword and attacks his master. Like Iago, both Cornwall and Regan are outraged. "A peasant stand up thus?" she cries and runs him through from behind before her husband can finish him off. It is all over in a moment (except as the other servants exchange shocked confidences afterward), but it recalls Christ's words at his entry into Jerusalem: "I tell you that, if these should hold their peace, the stones would immediately cry out." Where in literature do the stones come closer to crying out than here? And surely God must see in such an act some reason for going on with the world.

II

Shakespeare has not anywhere completely formularized what he considered the desirable qualities in a man, but Ophelia laments the overthrow of the courtier, soldier, and scholar in Hamlet's supposed madness, and it is clear that she has admired all three aspects. Henry V is more specific in his lamentation over the downfall of the traitors Cambridge, Scroop, and Grey:

Show men dutiful?
Why, so didst thou. Seem they grave and learned?
Why, so didst thou. Come they of noble family?
Why, so didst thou. Seem they religious?
Why, so didst thou. Or are they spare in diet,
Free from gross passion or of mirth or anger,
Constant in spirit, not swerving with the blood,
Garnish'd and deck'd in modest complement,
Not working with the eye without the ear,
And but in purged judgement trusting neither?

If we seek examples of Shakespeare's idea of a fine young man, surely we need search no further than Bassanio,[4] Romeo, and

4 A number of modern writers have seen Bassanio as a fortune hunter; this is an excellent example of what Stoll called anachronism in Shakespeare criticism, but

Orlando, and the one thing they all have in common is the same kind of gentle, considerate courtesy that has been attributed to Shakespeare himself. Romeo, not Paris. Paris is, to be sure, a model young man, but he is also what we used to call "an Arrow collar advertisement"; there is no indication that he ever in his life admired anything that did not come to him with the stamp "approved" upon it or failed to admire anything that did.[5] Even in *Love's Labour's Lost*, which, as has already been noted, is not the gentlest of Shakespeare's plays, Maria is made to lament a certain lack of courtesy in Longaville:

> Nothing becomes him ill that he would well.
> The only soil of his fair virtue's gloss,
> If virtue's gloss will stain with any soil,
> Is a sharp wit match'd with too blunt a will;
> Whose edge hath power to cut, whose will still wills
> It should none spare that come within his power.

It is clear that Hamlet too had Romeo's courtesy, but we never see Hamlet in his normal state; we can only catch glimpses of what he was like before his world fell to pieces around him, in his intercourse with Rosencrantz and Guildenstern, who did not deserve his friendship, and with the Players; moreover, the old story which Shakespeare inherited and which he reworked sometimes thrusts the courteous Renaissance gentleman far to the rear of the savage avenger.

Bassanio's withers are unwrung unless we insist upon applying standards which have no place in the thought of his time nor in the kind of romantic literature in which he exists. If he is not Portia's equal, he would be the first to grant it; that he loves her sincerely there is no doubt at all, and his choice of the right casket is not chance but the inevitable result of his unselfish understanding of life and love. The psychology of the time recognized three levels of judgment—sense and appetite, judgment and knowledge, understanding and will. All three are represented by Portia's suitors. Morocco chooses by the exterior view; Arragon has knowledge but lacks understanding and is blinded by self-love; only Bassanio responds to the challenge and gladly grants the lover's obligation to give and hazard all. See Charles Read Baskervill, "Bassanio as an Ideal Lover," *The Manly Anniversary Studies* (UCP, 1923).

[5] As usual, Shakespeare says all this best by the way he writes. Compare the empty rhetoric he puts into Paris' mouth in Act V, Scene 3, with the words he gives Romeo. Paris actually gets only one good line, his reference to the churchyard "being loose, unfirm, with digging up of graves."

If Shakespeare was interested in good men, he was also interested in good rulers, and he differentiates clearly between good rulers and bad. Richard II repels us through his cruelty to the helpless Gaunt, his whining, and the monstrous self-worship which will not even stop short of comparing him to Christ[6] and making God Almighty his ally. King Claudius in *Hamlet* is an extremely able man, but his fundamental harshness and lack of consideration for others comes through in his very first encounter with Hamlet in Act I. We may not all admire Henry V as much as Shakespeare intended us to admire him (of which more later, in another connection), but there can be no question that, however he acquired his knowledge, he does understand human nature. And we have already seen that even when a ruler has as little ruling to do in one of Shakespeare's plays as has Theseus in *A Midsummer Night's Dream* the dramatist still carefully considers his desirable qualities as a man and as a ruler and the connection between them.

Shakespeare knew—and he shows us in such figures as Malvolio —that self-love and overwhelming conceit may lead even a good man astray and deliver him over into the power of those who are in many ways inferior to himself. Obviously he did not trust to the poetic temperament for salvation (and this, surely, shows his capacity for disinterested self-judgment), since he gave it abundantly not only to Richard II but also to Macbeth. He knew that a great man, like Coriolanus, may be wrecked by pride, or, like Macbeth, swallowed up in the quagmires of evil because he used immoral means to gratify his ambition. He knew also that so high-minded a man as Othello may become a "gull," a "dolt," as "ignorant as dirt," if he allows passion to becloud his reason. He was fond of juxtapositions and confrontations between opposed types of men, as Brutus and Cassius or Antony and Octavius. In the first case, idealism stands over against practical judgment. We

[6]   Did they not sometimes cry, "All hail" to me?
So Judas did to Christ; but He, in twelve,
Found truth in all but one; I, in twelve thousand, none.

Perhaps a good mathematician might figure out just how much more wronged than Christ this made Richard!

respect Brutus when he refuses to allow Antony to be cut down with Caesar, but he reveals a fatal over-confidence when he supposes it safe to permit Antony to speak at Caesar's funeral, provided only he, Brutus, may speak first and tell the mob what to believe! Brutus is no match for Antony, but later, when that rabble-rouser is pitted against the machinelike efficiency of Octavius, he himself is hopelessly outclassed in his turn.

There are problems of course, and there are instances where we cannot but ask ourselves whether our response to a character is quite what the author intended. What, for example, of Proteus in *The Two Gentlemen of Verona*, who is both an unfaithful lover and a treacherous friend? He deserves much worse than he gets, and in a tragedy he would certainly have received it. But would Shakespeare have let him off as easily as he does even in a comedy if he had seemed quite the rat to him that he does to us? And what of Gratiano in *The Merchant of Venice*? Shakespeare makes it clear that both Antonio and Bassanio are aware of his faults (consider the shocking, insulting implications of the question Bassanio asks him when he reports having won Nerissa: "And do you, Gratiano, mean good faith?"), but both are on terms of close friendship with him, and there is no reason to believe that they found him altogether egregious. A more difficult case is that of Mercutio in *Romeo and Juliet*. I am aware that some critics have found him so attractive as to believe that if Shakespeare had not killed him, he would have killed the play, but this seems imperceptive. Except for his energy, Mercutio has few attractions; the imaginative Queen Mab speech is an aria, virtually detached from the action, and one cannot even be sure that Shakespeare intended it to reflect Mercutio's individual imagination; if it had not been for his unauthorized intervention, Romeo might have escaped the duel with Tybalt and, conceivably, his tragedy.[7] There is some-

---

[7] I wrote my remarks about Mercutio before I had seen Tucker Brooke's comments on that character in his *Essays on Shakespeare and Other Elizabethans* (YUP, 1948). Brooke found Mercutio's speeches almost entirely concerned with two subjects—smut and fencing. "So much has not often been made of smut and fencing; but these are rather trite materials out of which to construct the full character of a Renaissance princeling."

thing of this same brashness in Benedick and more of it in the Bastard of *King John*, yet his passionate expressions of English patriotism were certainly intended to please the audience.

We know that Shakespeare respected money and in the course of his life earned a good deal of it, but we have no reason to suppose that he ever acquired any in a questionable way. His lovers, however, are not above careful consideration of their market value. In *The Merry Wives of Windsor* Fenton tells Anne Page of her father,

> He doth object that I am too great of birth;
> And that, my state being gall'd with my expense,
> I seek to heal it only by his wealth.
> Besides these, other bars he lays before me,
> My riots past, my wild societies;
> And tells me 'tis a thing impossible
> I should love thee but as a property.

Clearly, this is not a very admirable young man from any point of view. Even in avowing his love for Anne, he must tell her

> Albeit I will confess thy father's wealth
> Was the first motive that I woo'd thee, Anne.

Fenton is not in himself very important, but similar questions arise elsewhere. As I have already tried to show, Bassanio truly loves Portia, but I am afraid he also *needs* her money. And what shall be said of Petruchio? It may well be that he *comes* to love Katherine; it has even been argued that his taming process results in the salvation of the nobler Katherine from herself ("marry, peace it bodes, and love, and quiet life"), but he makes up his mind to marry her before he has even seen her.

> Signor Hortensio, 'twixt such friends as we
> Few words suffice; and therefore, if you know
> One rich enough to be Petruchio's wife,
> As wealth is burden to my wooing dance,
> Be she as foul as was Florentius' love,

As old as Sybil, and as curst and shrewd
As Socrates' Xanthippe, or a worse,
She moves me not, or not removes, at least,
Affection's edge in me, were she as rough
As are the swelling Adriatic seas,
I come to wive it wealthily in Padua;
If wealthily, then happily, in Padua.

Benedick, too, insists on a wealthy wife: "Rich shall she be . . . ."

Graver questions are raised by the terrible scene in *Much Ado About Nothing* in which Claudio shames and repudiates Hero at the altar because he has believed monstrous slander about her. It is not only because we know she is innocent that this shocks us; Claudio's conduct would place him beyond the pale even if she were guilty. Probably, like Posthumus planning to have Imogen killed and Othello when he kills Desdemona, Claudio is in a measure plot-ridden here, yet within the action itself the Friar has sense enough to know that things are not what they seem, and the reaction of Beatrice to Claudio's conduct is much like our own. Hero's father Leonato, however, does not make up his mind to believe in his daughter until the very last act, when he rants and raves like an idiot, after having previously done everything in his power to worsen the situation as much as possible.

The defense of Hero by Beatrice gives us a woman's view of such matters, and this is not the only passage in which Shakespeare shows himself capable of looking at a man-woman situation through the woman's eyes. When Portia unfolds to Nerissa her plans for their visit to Venice as a lawyer and his clerk, she shows that there was not much about the young Renaissance gallant that she did not understand. The wry knowledge of Cressida (*Troilus and Cressida*, I, 3:312–21) and of Diana (*All's Well That Ends Well*, IV, 2:16–19) has been more dearly bought, but it is Rosalind who sums up the whole situation with the greatest eloquence and pathos. When, in the mock-wooing scene in the forest, Orlando promises to love "for ever and a day," she replies sadly,

Say 'a day,' without the 'ever.' No, no, Orlando. Men are April

71

when they woo, December when they wed; maids are May when they are maids, but the sky changes when they are wives.

III

We seem now to have shifted the emphasis from men to women, which of course involves the whole matter of sex and moral standards in Shakespeare.[8] In the old days, when modern literature was still discreet, the dramatist's sexual frankness was a count against him in many quarters, and his texts were always

---

[8] Since many of the sonnets seem to be addressed to a young man, it was no doubt inevitable that some critics should find homosexuality in Shakespeare. There is no justification whatever for this; with him passion is always heterosexual. The relationship between Achilles and Patroclus in *Troilus and Cressida* was not of his making, and it is presented most unsympathetically. "Poor lady," says Viola, upon becoming aware that Olivia has fallen in love with her as Cesario, "Poor lady, she were better love a dream." Even Slender specifically disclaims homosexual attraction in the mating mix-ups at the end of *The Merry Wives of Windsor*. But the prime piece of evidence is in Sonnet 20:

> And for a woman wert thou first created;
> Till Nature, as she wrought thee, fell a-doting,
> And by addition me of thee defeated
> By adding one thing to my purpose nothing.
>   But since she prick'd thee out for women's pleasure,
>   Mine be thy love, and thy love's use their treasure.

To which "The Passionate Pilgrim," XVIII (if it be Shakespeare's) adds:

> Were kisses all the joys in bed,
> One woman would another wed.

All this seems the more significant in view of the importance of the male friendship theme in Shakespeare's plays: Antonio and Bassanio, Brutus and Cassius, Romeo and Mercutio, Hamlet and Horatio, Sebastian and Antonio in *Twelfth Night*, etc. "I do adore thee so," says Antonio to Sebastian; few modern playwrights would permit themselves such a line with innocent intention. The Renaissance was fond of debating the respective claims of love between the sexes and friendship between members of the same sex, but when the palm of nobility was awarded to the latter, it was likely to be for the very reason that passion was not involved. Shakespeare has fun with this in the court scene of *The Merchant of Venice*, where both Bassanio and Gratiano assure Antonio, to the accompaniment of wry comment by their unrecognized wives, that he is much dearer to them than they are, but the Renaissance attitude appears seriously, I think, only at the end of *The Two Gentlemen of Verona*, where Valentine offers to relinquish Silvia to the worthless Proteus ("All that was mine in Silvia I give thee") as if she were a cargo to be reassigned. And this is not one of the passages which support Jonson's idea of Shakespeare as being "not of an age but for all time."

bowdlerized when prepared for school use or polite reading and when the plays were performed.[9] It is true that Shakespeare sometimes makes dramatic use of a sex-obsessed imagination. The whole of *Troilus and Cressida* is steeped in lust—"war and lechery confound all." Thersites is an animated scab, and Pandarus' tag-line at the end of the play is appalling. The Bastard in *King John*, though less appalling, is at least extremely coarse. Iago's imagination, too, is consistently debauched. "A lust of the blood and a permission of the will" is all he knows of love, and he suspects every one he knows, which is one of the reasons why it is hard to believe that all who know him, including his own wife, should think him "honest." Both Lear and Timon are sex-obsessed in their decline—if the king does not need the good apothecary to bring him an ounce of civet to sweeten his imagination by the time he calls for it, the reader certainly does—but in both cases the obsession is associated with disgust, not allure, and in Lear's daughters it becomes a force for monstrous evil.

Sexual frankness, however, is not confined to evil or deranged characters. See the coarse jesting between Hamlet and Rosencrantz and Guildenstern, the insults Hamlet hurls against the helpless Ophelia in the play scene, Petruchio's wooing of Katherine, and the scene between Lorenzo, Jessica, and Launcelot in *The Merchant of Venice* (III, 5). Leonato's reply to Benedick's query about Hero's parentage (*Much Ado*, I, 1) is an insult not only to Benedick but to Leonato's dead wife as well. In *Henry V*, the king invites the French princess to breed a boy by him even before she has accepted his suit, and some rather coarse jesting about sex follows, though the French queen Isabella is idealistic.

[9] I shall never forget how shocked I was when as a youngster I heard the ultra-fastidious E. H. Sothern permit Hamlet to send the word "whore" over the footlights. But in the last performance of *Romeo and Juliet* it was my misfortune to witness, all the bawdy lines were in place and all shouted at least twice as loud as anything else in the play. The critics and biographers too have changed, even since Middleton Murry assured us that from "country matters" we were, "thank Heaven . . . never far away in Shakespeare" (*Shakespeare* [HB, 1936]). In the early twenties, Joseph Quincy Adams was accused of trying to prove Shakespeare a model young man, but some more recent biographers are sent into such paroxysms of delight over his having "fornicated," as they believe, with Anne Hathaway that they suggest nothing so much as a dirty little boy spitting out forbidden words on the playground.

It will be seen that some of these scenes involve women. Cleopatra's talk is always pretty free, and except for brothel scenes, or those involving brothel characters, probably the bawdiest scene in Shakespeare in which women participate is *Antony and Cleopatra*, I, 2, which is of course in character. The same excuse might be made for the indelicate talk between Cressida and Pandarus but not for that between Helena and Parolles (*All's Well*, I, 1), and the Countess even tolerates indelicacy from that "foul-mouthed and calumnious knave," her clown. Perhaps Rosalind's bantering with Orlando in the forest might be excused as her notion of how a gay young blade talks, but there are other passages in *As You Like It* which cannot thus be explained away. Rosalind shows no resentment of Touchstone's bawdry nor of Celia's coarse reference to putting "a man in your belly." Julia's language toward the close of Act I, Scene 2 of *The Two Gentlemen of Verona* is much more discreet than Celia's, but it leaves no doubt as to what she is thinking about. Modern readers fail to catch the insult involved in Benedick's accusing Beatrice of having stolen her wit out of the *Hundred Merry Tales* (to which she responds by calling him an ale-house jester); this work was not considered proper reading matter for a lady. And even the aristocratic Portia allows herself to be drawn into some indecorous jesting about the rings in the last act of *The Merchant of Venice*.[10]

There are many other passages in Shakespeare, however, which, though frankly sexual, cannot be called bawdy because no innuendo (whether for comic or erotic purposes) is intended. Hermia tells Theseus she will surrender her "virgin patent" only to the man she loves; Miranda observes to her father that "good wombs have borne bad sons" and tells Ferdinand that she will "die your maid" if he does not marry her. Perdita defines the conditions under which she would have a youth breed by her in a conversation with (of all people) Polixenes, and even the child Mamilius is told that his pregnant mother "rounds apace" and "is

---

[10] The fullest treatment of this element in Shakespeare is now Eric Partridge, *Shakespeare's Bawdy: A Literary and Psychological Essay and a Comprehensive Glossary* (Du, 1948).

spread of late/ Into a goodly bulk." There is also a reasonable amount of sexual imagery. Hotspur fears that the devil and mischance may "look big/ Upon the maidenhead of our affairs," and the fairy Titania sees the sails of ships at sea "conceive/ And grow big-bellied with the wanton wind." In Sonnet 97 we read of

> The teeming autumn, big with rich increase,
> Bearing the wanton burden of the prime,
> Like widow'd wombs after their lords' decease.

The interesting thing about all this is that Shakespeare's great lovers should have been kept so wholly free of bawdry. *Romeo and Juliet* is surely the purest and sweetest of all the great love stories of the world, and though the play has plenty of bawdry in it, the hero and heroine are not associated with it.[11] Capulet himself testifies that Verona "brags" of Romeo as "a virtuous and well-govern'd youth," and we should know this even if he did not tell us. It is no accident that he stops Mercutio's Queen Mab fantasy short at the precise point where it turns toward bawdry, and Juliet "stints" her Nurse in her mother's presence just after she has told a mildly indelicate anecdote of the girl's childhood. Outside Capulet's orchard after the ball, Benvolio warns Mercutio that Romeo will be angry if he hears his bawdy talk. When Romeo himself, in the balcony scene, innocently asks, "O, wilt thou leave me so unsatisfied?" Juliet bluntly replies, "What satisfaction canst thou have to-night?" Once sure of her unalterable commitment, she moves to marry her love; the thought of premarital intercourse may occur to the Friar and the Nurse; it never occurs to the lovers themselves.

This is by no means the only reason we may fairly judge the Shakespearean drama to be less heavily sexed than a superficial examination might indicate. It is true that in *Venus and Adonis* as in the Sonnets increase is a duty, with his passionate horse setting a good example to the chaste Adonis, but this is certainly

---

[11] Juliet's soliloquy in Act III, Scene 2 is of course one of the most passionate speeches in Shakespeare, but there is no bawdry in it nor the faintest suggestion of any.

not the dominant Shakespearean point of view. A man is not an animal, and his passions must be guided by reason.[12] Compare the plays with their sources and it will appear clearly that Shakespeare again and again softens, omits, or refines the sexual motivation. Even in a play like *The Comedy of Errors*, he cleans up both the Antipholi and softens the shrewish wife, while the role of the Courtezan is played down to such an extent that one can perceive no reason why she should be called a courtesan at all. In Barnabe Riche's *Apolonius and Silla*, which is one of the sources of *Twelfth Night*, the Sebastian character spends the night with Olivia and gets her with child; later when she claims Silla (Viola) as her husband, the girl strips to reveal her sex. In Bandello the plot against Hero originates in the jealousy of a former rejected suitor, and in Cinthio's *Hecatommithi* the villainy of the ensign is rooted in his unrequited love for the Moor's wife, who, incidentally, is beaten to death with a sandbag by the ensign while the Moor looks on! Finally, it has been pointed out again and again that if Shakespeare's last plays were influenced by the new trends in drama which came in with Beaumont and Fletcher, he still kept himself free of the moral laxity associated with it in these and other writers.[13]

[12] It is possible that *Venus and Adonis* may be more representative of the known tastes of the Earl of Southampton, to whom it was dedicated, than of Shakespeare's own. Even if we do not go along with Harold C. Goddard's view that "on the parabolic level," the poem is "one of the most powerful protests ever written against too early initiation into sexual experience" (*The Meaning of Shakespeare* [UCP, 1951]), one may still be impressed by Peter Quennell and others finding its "erotic content" slight compared to that of similar works by Marlowe, Nashe, and others. "It has a minimal effect upon the modern reader's senses," says Quennell, "and, at least in so far as its subject is love or lust, seldom touches the imagination." And he adds, "Perhaps his theme was uncongenial to the poet" (*Shakespeare: A Biography* [World Publishing Company, 1963]). It is interesting that having written *Venus and Adonis*, Shakespeare should have turned next to the much more moral though no less sexually motivated *Rape of Lucrece*.

[13] "In only six of his [Shakespeare's] thirty-eight plays is an act of fornication or adultery, as distinct from the suspicion of such acts, really encompassed; and when these plays are read in the light of the anterior literature to which they relate, the fact appears as simply astonishing. Shakespeare was almost as determined an expurgator as Bowdler. He is practically the only writer who omits the Jane Shore episode in treating the lives of Edward the Fourth and Richard the Third, and practically the only one who refrains from punishing jealous husbands in comedy by making their wives unfaithful" Alfred Harbage, *As They Liked It*, pp. x–xi. See, fur-

76

Goldwin Smith long ago observed that there is no Don Juan among Shakespeare's heroes.[14] Sonnet 66 speaks eloquently of "maiden virtue rudely strumpeted," and in 2 *Henry VI* "to force a spotless virgin's chastity" is one of the unpardonable sins. Shakespeare's girls come to the altar virgins;[15] as for the antecedent "sex lives" of his heroes, about which certain commentators have over-curiously and somewhat pruriently exercised themselves, Stoll and others have shown that all such considerations are irrelevant. ("The only important questions in his plays left open, except through hastiness and carelessness, are those put by the critics themselves."[16]) It is true that Isabella in *Measure for Measure* is the only heroine who inclines toward asceticism, and this only at the beginning of the play; when the Duke chooses her as his wife, she voices no objection. One grants that Isabella must be incomprehensible to an audience which does not understand the traditional Jewish-Christian attitude toward chastity ("Puritanism" has nothing to do with the case), but the generally sensible M. M. Reese is absurd when he writes that it was her "religious vows" which prevented her from saving Claudio as Angelo proposed, and that "her tragedy was that, while she could plead mercy for Claudio's fault, her profession forbade her to win it by falling into the same fault herself." Can one imagine any other Shakespearean heroine accepting Claudio's offer? and could she possibly have retained the respect of the audience if she had done so? There is no "tragedy" in *Measure for Measure*: Isabella tricks Angelo precisely as Helena, who has no "profession," tricks Bertram in *All's Well*. And Reese himself inconsistently recognizes all this when he continues: "Dramatically it was a superb 'situation,' but it was

ther, his "Shakespeare as Expurgator," in *Shakespeare and the Rival Tradition* (M, 1952).

[14] *Shakespeare the Man: An Attempt to Find Traces of the Dramatist's Character in his Dramas* (D, 1900).

[15] The only exception occurs in the case of Claudio and Juliet in *Measure for Measure*, and since their difficulties are purely practical, not moral, nor their conduct very shocking by Elizabethan standards, their repentance seems greatly overdone. Even the "enskied and sainted" Isabella cries, "O, let him marry her" when the couple's predicament is explained to her.

[16] Elmer Edgar Stoll, *From Shakespeare to Joyce* ... (D, 1944), 148–49.

also in harmony with Shakespeare's consistent unwillingness to involve his characters in unlawful love."

Again let me say that all this has very little to do with what moderns think of as Puritanism. In *Love's Labour's Lost* the proposed asceticism of the King and his friends gets short shrift; in *Measure for Measure* Pompey asks Escalus whether he intends to geld and splay all the youth of Vienna. The Puritans were not ascetics in matters of sex but legalists, and it looks very much as though Shakespeare may have agreed with them on this point. Whoring and tavern-roistering are not presented admiringly or alluringly in *Measure for Measure* nor yet in *Pericles* nor the *Henry IV* plays. It is true that the dramatist's humor does not desert him, but even for Falstaff the end is disease and death. The very first words he speaks in *2 Henry IV* refer to his disease; the terrible emphasis cannot possibly be accidental. Doll Tearsheet too is diseased, and at last even Mistress Quickly must be completely degraded. The terrible "lust in action" sonnets are hardly more uncompromising.

Both Hamlet and the Shepherd in *The Winter's Tale* think of passion as peculiarly a sin of youth. The adultery of Claudius and the Queen is presented as a shameful thing. Laertes and Polonius both misjudge Hamlet by seeing him as one like unto themselves, and Polonius' own servant is shocked by his master's low standards in the scene where he is set to work spying upon Laertes. The melancholy of Jaques in *As You Like It* seems, like that of Sansjoy in *The Faerie Queene,* the result of his own early excesses. Edward IV is a lusty fribble who jeopardizes the fortunes of the whole House of York by insisting upon marrying (and enjoying) Lady Grey just as soon as he has been stimulated by her, even while negotiations for the hand of the French princess are in progress. In *King Lear* the handling of the sin of Gloucester which produced his villainous bastard son seems quite Victorian. "I stumbled when I saw," he says after his blinding, and Edgar remarks,

> The gods are just, and of our pleasant vices,
> Make instruments to plague us.

The dark and vicious place where thee he got
Cost him his eyes.

I do not claim either that this statement conveys the complete
meaning of the play or that Shakespeare would have been willing
to go to the stake to maintain its implications, but it *is* a part of
the play and, taken together with the other passages I have cited,
it cannot be altogether without significance.[17]

Antony and Cleopatra has seemed to some an exception to all
this, and Shaw found the play "intolerable" because, though
faithful in its portrayal of the end result of debauchery, it finally
strains all the resources of pathos and sublimity "to persuade
foolish spectators that the world was well lost by the twain." But
this is a superficial reading. Shakespeare does not "blame" Cleopatra as Plutarch does, and he omits some of Plutarch's most unpleasant touches. Yet the inevitable doom shadows the lovers
from the beginning. Shakespeare's Cleopatra is a magnificent
woman but not a good one, and whomever she fascinates, she
never fascinated her creator in any sense which implies that she
beclouded his judgment. Says E. E. Stoll:

> The dramatist has despite his sympathy "held the balance
> even." He has secured our interest without prejudicing the
> moral cause. . . . He shrewdly remembers [the] illicit basis [of
> the love of Antony and Cleopatra], its suspicions, jealousies,
> and resentments; and at her best Cleopatra is fain to call herself
> a wife.[18] Here is no glorification, in mediaeval style, of illicit
> love at the expense of the married state, whether on the part of
> the lovers or their friends. These are no Lancelot and Guine-
> vere, Tristram and Iseult. For that matter, there are none such
> in Shakespeare.[19]

[17] I must say, however, that Malcolm's self-arraignment for monstrous lust when
testing Macduff's loyalty in *Macbeth* (IV, 3) does not seem much more convincing
to me than it did to Macduff, and I do not believe that much is accomplished by
it. Macduff's own standards in this matter seem fairly "liberal," but we have had
no indication elsewhere that inordinate lust was one of Macbeth's sins.

[18] "Husband I come!/ Now to that name my courage prove my title!" (V,
2:290–91). At an earlier stage she had asked scornfully of Octavia, "What says the
married woman?" (EW's note.)

[19] *Poets and Playwrights* . . . (University of Minnesota Press, 1930).

Stoll finds further that "the poet restrains himself in the matter of voluptuousness and erotic coloring." His "Egyptian passions," though "real enough," are not "near and nude, but keep the cool, serene distance of art." And he concludes that Shakespeare "was conventional in his notions and opinions," and that "though not a Puritan," he resembled Tolstoy in that "his presentation of character was far wider than his intellectual scope."

These impressions are supported, I think, by the omnipresence of moralizing in Shakespeare, as in English literature generally. Sometimes, as outstandingly with Hamlet, it is justified by the naturally generalizing tendency of a philosophical mind, but Shakespeare needs no such justification. Macbeth's "tomorrow and tomorrow" speech after the death of his wife has of course been colored by his own experience; he describes life as he has lived it.[20] But Tarquin moralizes on his way to rape Lucrece, and Iago's praise of reputation, whose importance he had previously dismissed along with that of all other nonmaterial things, though as hypocritical in his mouth as "This is the fruits of whoring" after Roderigo has been killed, is noble enough when quoted out of context. The platitudinizing of Friar Laurence in *Romeo and Juliet* may appeal primarily to rudimentary minds like that of the Nurse, who could have stayed in his cell all night to hear such counsel, but if Shakespeare had been as much bored by Laurence as some modern commentators are, one can only say that he turned the joke on his audiences and even upon himself by giving the friar such space as he did; as a matter of fact, Hamlet himself is almost as trying (though not at such length) in his apology to Laertes (V, 2:237-55). It may well be that Shakespeare did not set quite the same valuation as we do upon what is called "originality."

But though Shakespeare's girls are "good," they are ruled by love, and he seems to take it for granted that if a girl is really in

[20] "Macbeth may say that 'Life is a tale told by an idiot,' but the play of *Macbeth* is not a tale of a world run by an idiot. It is a tale of a world of clearly defined moral law, in which Macbeth and his particular actions meet with the indestructible and the universal"—Lily B. Campbell, *Shakespeare's "Histories," Mirrors of Elizabethan Policy* (The Huntington Library, 1947), 7.

love, she will marry the man who has won her heart, no matter what may stand in the way. Even parental disobedience appears so slight a fault in this connection as hardly to be worth thinking of. The trifling Fenton can hardly be considered a chorus character, but he surely expresses the sense of *The Merry Wives of Windsor,* and of its author, when he defends Anne Page and himself in the following terms:

> Hear the truth of it.
> You would have married her most shamefully,
> Where there was no proportion held in love.
> The truth is, she and I, long since contracted,
> Are now so sure that nothing can dissolve us.
> The offence is holy that she hath committed;
> And this deceit loses the name of craft,
> Of disobedience, or unduteous title,
> Since therein she doth evitate and shun
> A thousand irreligious cursed hours
> Which forced marriage would have brought upon her.

An "arranged" marriage is, then, a greater offense than any mistaken choice which has been honestly made. Juliet would have accepted that and Desdemona and Imogen and even Hermia in the half-fairy world of *A Midsummer Night's Dream.* Desdemona breaks through the race barrier—"To fall in love with what she fear'd to look on!"—and Imogen defies a king. Cordelia, too, is sure that when she weds, her husband must in large measure fill up the place in her life which has hitherto been occupied by her father.[21]

Shakespeare created the most enchanting women in literature, and it would be difficult to believe that he did not understand or

---

[21] The only obedient heroine of any consequence in Shakespeare is Ophelia, who has been roundly scolded again and again for not having helped Hamlet in a plot of whose existence she was never made aware. So far as Ophelia knows or could know, Hamlet was a lover who went mad. As for her lie in Act III, Scene 3 ("At home, my lord"), no defense is needed. One does not tell the truth to mad people—unless one is mad oneself. But see Alfred Harbage, *Conceptions of Shakespeare,* 128–30, for a rather startling demonstration that Shakespeare's good characters in general are not bound to any narrow conception of truth-telling.

respond to them. According to *The Rape of Lucrece* women are wax to men's marble, and Duke Orsino of *Twelfth Night* considers them emotionally shallow, but the plays in general do not bear out these views.[22] If Biron of *Love's Labour's Lost* has little faith in female chastity, Hamlet, even in his disillusionment, puts women on a higher plane than men, and cannot understand why such as Ophelia could wish to become a breeder of sinners. Even when Othello has been driven half mad by Iago's lies, his faith in Desdemona revives momentarily at the sight of her—"If she be false, [O, then heaven mocks] itself!"—and if he had only had sense enough to trust his intuition, the tragedy might yet have been averted. Troilus himself, at the end of the play, is not willing to damn all women for Cressida.[23]

Of course there are much worse women than Cressida in Shakespeare. The "Amazonian trull" and "she-wolf of France," Margaret of Anjou, in the *Henry VI* plays, is worse than Lady Macbeth, for she herself stabs York, and she is an unfaithful wife besides. There are women's scolding matches in both *Richard II* and *Titus Andronicus*, where even Lavinia is degraded by her

[22] C. R. Baskervill used to point out that the heroines of the early comedies reflected the accomplishments of the Renaissance lady and were far more intellectual than the men associated with them.

[23] Cressida is of course a "bad" heroine, but Shakespeare had no choice here; she had been degraded for him by the whole literary tradition which had developed since Chaucer's time. But she is not presented quite unsympathetically in her scenes with Troilus, and it is at least questionable whether her vulgarity upon her arrival in the Greek camp and her subsequent disloyalty to her lover have been adequately prepared for. Personally I must confess that the one leading Shakespearean heroine who does not quite come off for me is Beatrice in *Much Ado*. Possibly the reason may be that I have never seen her presented by a first-class actress, and if I could have seen Ellen Terry in the role (reputedly her greatest) I might well feel otherwise. As it is, I find Beatrice before her awakening rather less than more attractive than Katherine the Shrew. She is a railing woman, and if she is not overcome by passion, she is merely showing off, which is worse. There is something vulgar about her sparring with Benedick all through the first part of the play, and if she appeals more than Katherine, I think this is mainly because Shakespeare has lavished greater stylistic splendor upon her. I do not think my reaction here wholly idiosyncratic, for *Much Ado* has not held its place in the theater alongside the other first-rate comedies. Sothern and Marlowe produced it, but it always drew less well for them than the other items in their repertoire. As for Katherine herself, all I can say is that she improves upon acquaintance. Dr. Furness once cautioned Julia Marlowe: "Do not forget, dear Julia, that Bianca is the real shrew." The last act of the play lends some support to this view.

participation in one, and the wooing of Anne by the future
Richard III dramatizes the conventional medieval notion of the
weak woman. Constance in *King John* is not evil, but she is one of
the unwisest loving mothers on record; it must have been almost
worth Arthur's dying to avoid having her smother him further.

The Shakespearean heroine is beautiful, but since her creator
was a dramatist, not a novelist, he could not describe her appearance in detail. Benedick says "her hair shall be of what colour
it please God," and it may be that Shakespeare agreed with him,
though he makes Portia a blonde, giving her, perhaps, that particular rich shade of blonde hair which, because of its rarity, was
greatly prized in Italy and which we see in some Renaissance portraits. The one thing we can be sure of is that he was sensitive to
the charm of a beautiful and well-placed voice; as Lear says of
Cordelia:

> Her voice was ever soft,
> Gentle, and low; an excellent thing in woman.

Yet in the ordinary sense he did not idealize women, and there
was not much about feminine (or, for that matter, masculine)
vagaries that he did not know. His references to false hair and cosmetics (whose use in his day was not wholly limited to women)
are not admiring, and they are rather significant as coming from
a writer who so seldom commits himself on personal preferences
and prejudices.[24]

From the modern point of view, the lack of sexual pride sometimes shown by his heroines is a more serious matter, but I find no
reason for supposing that Shakespeare himself was aware of this.
Helena's unmaidenly behavior in forcing herself upon Demetrius
was of course required by the plot of *A Midsummer Night's
Dream*, but did she have to say,

> I am your spaniel, and, Demetrius,

---

[24] See *The Merchant of Venice*, III, 2:88–96; *Twelfth Night*, I, 5:287ff.; *Hamlet*, III, 1:148ff., 212–14; also Sonnet 68. Shakespeare's presumed view was not,
however, peculiar to him. Both Castiglione and Guazzo condemn cosmetics, and
the latter calls the woman who uses it a harlot.

> The more you beat me, I will fawn on you.
> Use me but as your spaniel, spurn me, strike me,
> Neglect me, lose me; only give me leave,
> Unworthy as I am, to follow you,

and could these lines have been written for her by a dramatist who squirmed over them quite as we do? The same thing appears in more aggravated form in another Helena's pursuit of Bertram in *All's Well* and in the Mariana episode of *Measure for Measure*. Both women get possession of a man's bed by a trick; under the highly artificial circumstances posited, neither has violated the moral standards of the time, but each surely has placed herself in a most undignified position. The only point at which any modern reader is at all likely to sympathize with that unconscionable cad Bertram is when he refuses to permit a wife whom he has not chosen to be thrust upon him, and Helena is a consenting partner to this scheme. It is true that she is a hundred times too good for him, but that is another matter. Why on earth did she want him? and why did Mariana want Angelo, knowing his worthlessness as she did?

Some critics have fancied that they discerned a certain weariness in Shakespeare's last plays, but I should say emphatically that if Shakespeare was tired of anything during the last years of his life, it was certainly not women. Imogen, Hermione, Perdita, Katherine of Aragon—if such as these cannot satisfy us, we had better not waste any more time with the human race. Hermione's iron reserve and sweet womanly dignity under monstrous and ridiculous accusation are overwhelming:

> Should a villain say so,
> The most replenish'd villain in the world,
> He were as much more villain; you, my lord,
> Do but mistake.
>
> How this will grieve you,
> When you shall come to clearer knowledge, that
> You thus have publish'd me! Gentle, my lord,

You scarce can right me throughly then to say
You did mistake.

              If I shall be condemn'd
Upon surmises, all proofs sleeping else
But what your jealousies awake, I tell you
'Tis rigour and not law.

In their context, these are surely among the great utterances not only of the feminine but of the human spirit. Hermione's daughter Perdita inherits her courage, as she proves by her words to Florizel after having been threatened by his father Polixines:

I was not much afeard; for once or twice
I was about to speak, and tell him plainly
The self-same sun that shines upon his court
Hides not his visage from our cottage, but
Looks on alike.

And Imogen's "False to his bed" speech in *Cymbeline* (III, 4) is perhaps the most touching thing the dramatist ever wrote.[25]

This brings us naturally to Shakespeare's portrayal of the relations between husbands and wives, in which, as every reader will recognize, he achieves almost the variety of nature itself. Antigonus in *The Winter's Tale* says a wife cannot be controlled by a husband, and in *A Midsummer Night's Dream* even Titania is what the Middle Ages called "unbuxom." Adriana in *The Comedy of Errors* is shrewish too, though less so than in the source, but she is also a woman of character, with a high ideal of marriage; her more winning but less idealistic sister Luciana accepts male supremacy without question and is even willing to wink at a little male infidelity if it will contribute to a quiet household. Beatrice promises to tame her wild heart to Benedick's

25 It is interesting that Posthumus should remark that in their marital relations, Imogen "restrained" him of his "lawful pleasure." Her great love for him then was not pre-eminently or even markedly sensual. This is the only glimpse we ever get of any Shakespearean heroine in the marriage bed. It is possible, however, that the statement was not intended to achieve anything more than to heighten our feeling of the insane jealousy Posthumus feels at this point toward Iachimo.

loving hand, and Emilia in *Othello* accepts her obligation to obey Iago, "but not now," she says, in the very special circumstances of the last act.

Petruchio's assertion of male supremacy over Katherine is brutal even if we grant that it was necessary for her welfare as well as his, and Katherine accepts it, along with all other aspects of "order" in her famous closing speech, which is about the strongest statement of the case for male supremacy in marriage that could have been made in Shakespeare's time. But what are we to say about such girls as Portia and Rosalind? (The gentle Viola, surely, could be no problem to anybody.) Will the men they marry never find themselves overmatched? Nothing surely could surpass Portia's frankness in her charge to Bassanio before he proceeds to his choice of the caskets, nor her joyous self-surrender when he has won her, nor her generosity, both financial and emotional, when their betrothal joy is rudely broken in upon by Antonio's crisis. But was she really able to keep her promise

> that her gentle spirit
> Commits itself to yours to be directed,
> As from her lord, her governor, her king?

No doubt she fully meant what she said. But in both the court scene and the comedy of the rings in the last act, we find her and Nerissa running their own show, with Bassanio and Gratiano following willingly along.[26]

In a class by herself among Shakespeare's wives is Lady Macbeth. Both Mrs. Siddons and Charlotte Cushman played her as a figure of dominating, baleful grandeur—a "fiend-like queen"—but Mrs. Siddons at least knew that she was imposing herself upon the character. When she thought about Lady Macbeth, she saw her as a small woman, physically frail, "possibly even fragile," whose courage contrasts strikingly with her slight physical resources, so that she soon breaks under the terrible strain she has

---

[26] St. John Ervine's comedy, *The Lady of Belmont* (1923), delightfully explores the married life of Bassanio and Portia, with special emphasis upon a later encounter with Shylock and Antonio.

imposed upon herself. She intended to kill Duncan herself, but when she came to his chamber she could not do so, for he resembled her father as he slept. Her "if he do bleed," when she goes back for the daggers Macbeth had stupidly left in the king's chambers, shows how little she knew about slaughter. She sees the blood then, and she goes on seeing it until the end of her life, when her mind breaks under the strain and she kills herself.

Her ambition was all for her husband, not, as in Holinshed, for herself. She is a loving wife—prosaic, unimaginative, materially-minded; if she had had an imagination, Duncan would never have died. Neither does she understand her husband; had she done so, she would not have been so foolish as to suppose that he could ever be happy in the path they chose to walk together.

Yet they do not walk it together, for he soon leaves her behind to walk it alone. She has no share in any of Macbeth's crimes except the first; "What's to be done?" she asks him before the murder of Banquo, but he does not tell her. What a world of weariness in her reply to his "What is the night?" after the banquet scene: "Almost at odds with morning, which is which." And from here she proceeds shortly to the tenderest line Shakespeare wrote for her: "You lack the season of all natures, sleep." She who was once his other self has been reduced to being his old nanny. Soon she will not even be that.

Women—and marriage—mean children. Children are not numerous in Shakespeare's plays, nor do they seem greatly to have stimulated his powers as an artist. The characteristic note of the Shakespearean child is pertness, as may be seen in Macduff's doomed son and in Mamilius of *The Winter's Tale*, and even, though now with an admixture of malevolence, in the young Duke of York in *Richard III* (II, 4 and III, 1), whose skillful baiting of his uncle Gloucester has provided such a golden opportunity for so many generations of little brats on the stage. I do not, however, mean to suggest that the Shakespearean child is ignoble. Young Lucius, of *Titus Andronicus*, is high-minded and capable of deep feeling, though, in such a play, the expression of his emotion must at times be unpleasantly savage. Even Macduff's son,

who appears in only one scene, has his moment of nobility in death, and we are evidently intended to regard Mamilius as a noble young prince indeed since he sickens and dies over the wrong inflicted upon his mother, Hermione. Except for Antigonus, he is the only character in *The Winter's Tale* who suffers quite irremediably.

Arthur in *King John* is a bird of another feather, coming pretty close to the angel child whom the nineteenth century was to love. A pawn between two viragoes—his mother and his grandmother —he cries,

> I would that I were low laid in my grave;
> I am not worth the coil that's made for me,

yet when he is taken prisoner his first thought is not for himself but for Constance: "O, this will make my mother die with grief!" But he is more like a little adult than a real child in Act IV, Scene 1, where he successfully begs Hubert to spare his eyes, and the same must be said of young Rutland, who is less fortunate when he pleads with Clifford for his life in 3 *Henry VI* (I, 3). Clarence's children in *Richard III* are far from childlike also when they cry:

> BOY.   Ah! aunt, you wept not for our father's death;
>   How can we aid you with our kindred tears?
> GIRL.   Our fatherless distress was left unmoan'd;
>   Your widow-dolour likewise be unwept!

We need to remember, however, that children *are* young adults in medieval and Renaissance art in general, and perhaps they were in life also, to a larger extent than we can easily realize now. Though Chaucer did remarkably well in "The Prioress's Tale," generally speaking it may still be said that the use of real children in literature, and especially as leading characters in literature intended for adults, is not a pre-Dickensian phenomenon. It may very well be, therefore, that what I have said about Shakespeare's children shows less about his personal attitude toward them than Manly and some of the earlier students of his personality believed.

It is interesting too that the Arthur of what we may tentatively call the source play, *The Troublesome Raigne of John King of England,* is much less pure and disinterested than Shakespeare's character. When Queen Elinor urges that Richard's will bars Arthur's succession, the child replies, without waiting for his elders to speak,

> But say there was, as sure there can be none,
> The law intends such testaments as void,
> When right descent can no way be impeacht,

so that even Constance cries, "Peace, Arthur, peace." Before Angiers he asks,

> Ye citizens of Angiers, are ye mute?
> Arthur or John, say which shall be your king?

And when the men of Angiers propose a compromise, he breaks in caustically,

> A proper peace, if such a motion hold;
> These kings bear arms for me, and for my right,
> And they shall share my lands to make them friends.

In short, the Arthur of *The Troublesome Raigne* behaves much like Edward Prince of Wales in 3 *Henry VI,* who, let us devoutly hope, is non-Shakespearean, but who is, in any case, one of the most obnoxious children in literature. When informed that he is to marry Warwick's daughter, he replies, with colossal egotism, "Yes, I accept her, for she well deserves it." For once, one must agree with Clarence—"Untutor'd lad, thou art too malapert"— and though nothing can excuse the boy's murder, one must admit that it yields much less pathos than it might have yielded with a different sort of victim.

One boy in Shakespeare suffers corruption at the hands of evil adult associates. This is Falstaff's page, who has "a good angel about him; but the devil blinds him too." The process is not shown in detail, but 2 *Henry IV,* II, 2 is not, in this connection, pleasant. Is this the same boy we meet again in *Henry V,* III, 2?

If so, he seems to be turning out rather better than we might have expected; perhaps the devil did not win after all. In any case, Shakespeare does not appear to have believed with Dickens's Mr. Hubble that children were "naterally wicious"; indeed there is an interesting passage in *The Winter's Tale* in which this is specifically denied. Looking back upon his childhood and that of Leontes together, Polixenes says,

> We were as twinn'd lambs that did frisk i' th' sun,
> And bleat the one at th' other. What we chang'd
> Was innocence for innocence; we knew not
> The doctrine of ill-doing, [no], nor dream'd
> That any did. Had we pursu'd that life,
> And our weak spirits ne'er been higher rear'd
> With stronger blood, we should have answer'd Heaven
> Boldly, "Not guilty"; the imposition clear'd
> Hereditary ours.

Whatever may be thought of Shakespeare's portraits of children, however, there can be no question that he observed them carefully, as he did every aspect of the life of the kitchen and the household, including the mother's and the nurse's activities in the home. He must, one would think, have been an intensely domestic man; it seems a pity that his work should have compelled one of his temperament to spend so much of his life away from his family in lodgings. He must have enjoyed his stays with the Mountjoys and the Davenants; no wonder he played Cupid for Mountjoy's daughter; no wonder that the Reverend Robert Davenant should afterward have declared that Shakespeare had kissed him as a child a hundred times. Perhaps the most interesting notation of child behavior is in Sonnet 143, where we see "the neglected child" who pursues the "careful housewife," herself pursuing "one of her feathered creatures broke away," a genre picture worthy of Chaucer, but Caroline Spurgeon and others have marshaled an array of figures and images based upon the domestic aspects of life which simply cannot be brushed away; there is no

questioning Shakespeare's interest in it.[27] He himself was the
father of two daughters and one son. The son was early lost and
his father's hope of founding a family along with him. There are
suggestions that Judith may in some ways have been a disappoint-
ment to him. With Susanna, who married Dr. Hall, all seems to
have been harmonious, as with her daughter Elizabeth, who first
married Thomas Nash, then, after his death, Sir John Barnard,
but who died without issue, so that when she went in 1670 the
direct Shakespeare line became extinct.[28]

IV

All this tells a good deal about what Shakespeare believed and
how he felt about the relations of men and women; about his own
actual conduct it tells us less. But there has been no lack of speculation in this area, and much of it has been silly.

It should be stated to begin with that the only woman with
whose name Shakespeare's can be certainly connected is the
woman he married, Anne Hathaway. He married her, aged twenty-
six, when he himself was only eighteen, by special license, after
only one asking of the banns, and six months later their daughter
Susanna was born. The suggestion that this was a "shotgun marriage" disturbed Victorian critics and editors greatly, but some of
the recent commentators seem to have found great comfort in it.
It may well be, however, that this comfort is insecurely grounded.
We simply do not know enough about the circumstances of
Shakespeare's marriage to be dogmatic about it. He *may* have
seduced Anne (or she *may* have seduced him), but we cannot be
sure that there was not a formal betrothal, the actual marriage
ceremony being, for some unknown reason, delayed until the
woman's condition made it seem advisable to delay no longer. In
other words, the difficulties involved may have been of a purely
practical nature, with no moral considerations involved. We know

[27] Spurgeon, *Shakespeare's Imagery* . . . , 113ff.; cf. Fripp, 435–36.
[28] See Joseph Quincy Adams, *A Life of William Shakespeare* (HM, 1923), Chs.
XXIV–XXVI, for an excellent account of these family matters.

of other cases in which something like this happened, and the parties concerned do not seem to have lost caste by it. We cannot *prove* that a formal betrothal existed, but neither can those who disbelieve in it prove that it did not. Perhaps the final grace in scholarship is to learn to admit invincible ignorance. And for many scholars it is apparently the hardest of all to acquire.[29]

The popular impression that Shakespeare's marriage was unhappy is sheer hypothesis; we have no facts which support it. We are not even sure that when he left for London he did not take his family with him. They were certainly in Stratford at a later date, and Shakespeare certainly spent some time in lodgings, but Stratford was always his base; no doubt he returned there whenever he was able; and he was still a comparatively young man when he came back for good, never to be separated from his family again. Leave the circumstances of the marriage out of it, and there is not the slightest suggestion anywhere that Anne Shakespeare ever bore anything but a sterling reputation. From the little we know of her, we get the impression of a quiet, retiring woman, devoted to her family, and of sound, even strict, moral principles. Tradition says she wished to be buried in the same grave with her husband (whom she outlived), but that this desire was frustrated because nobody cared to defy the mandate over his grave. She was buried beside him therefore, where unfortunately there was no doggerel to protect her, and when the time came, her remains were taken up and cast into the common boneyard.[30] As for the bequest of the "second best bed," which has occasioned so much unseemly mirth, this was probably Anne's own favorite bed, which her husband, possibly at her own request, wished to make sure could not be taken from her. We certainly need not draw the fantastic conclusion that this was all she received. Her share of the estate

[29] The best statement of the case in favor of a betrothal is in Adams, *Life,* 67ff.
[30]   Good friend, for Jesus' sake, forebear
       To dig the dust enclosed here:
       Blessed be the man that spares these stones,
       And cursed be he that moves my bones.
Let nobody ask why the world's greatest poet should have been buried under such doggerel. This is precisely the kind of "poetry" that sextons and gravediggers could understand. The inscription has "worked" now for more than three hundred years.

may well have been covered by widow's dower rights or in some
other way.

Was Shakespeare "faithful" to Anne during the time they spent
apart? Who can say? And since most people do not make a public
record of their transgressions, who can answer such a question
positively about any man—or woman? What we must say, however, is that we have no knowledge whatever of any infidelity upon
Shakespeare's part. He lived at one time in Shoreditch, perhaps
the most disreputable part of London, but John Aubrey records
that he "wouldn't be debauched" and that to this end, he declined
invitations to parties, pleading indisposition. His known associates
in the theater were serious, sober men of character, and such gossip as has been circulated about him turns out upon examination
to be the kind of filth that the greasy-minded circulate about
everybody whose name becomes a matter of public interest,
whether they know anything about him or not. Shakespeare himself fixed the type forever in Lucio of *Measure for Measure*.

Take, for example, the Manningham story, dating from 1602:

> Upon a time when Burbage played Richard III, there was a
> citizen . . . so far in liking with him that before she went from
> the play she appointed him to come that night unto her by the
> name of Richard III. Shakespeare, overhearing their conclusion,
> went before, was entertained, and at his game ere Burbage
> came. Then message being brought that Richard III was at the
> door, Shakespeare caused return to be made that William the
> Conqueror was before Richard III.

As H. C. Beeching has justly observed,[31] it is "upon a time" which
gives the key here. The yarn

> evidently belongs to the type of coarse and witty story always
> popular in England, of which every jest-book from the *Hundred
> Merry Tales* onward is full; but which no one troubles to be-
> lieve; or indeed would be likely to believe if he stopped to ask
> the question how the story came to be told.

[31] *The Character of Shakespeare*, British Academy, Annual Lecture, 1917. See
also his "The Benefit of the Doubt," in Israel Gollancz, ed., *A Book of Homage to
Shakespeare* (OUP, 1916).

The question here is not merely whether Shakespeare was capable of making, or even "horning in" upon, an assignation. There is more to it than that. Here, according to all reports, was one of the most "gentle," courteous, and reserved men of the Elizabethan age. Can one seriously think of him as calling himself "William the Conqueror" under the conditions postulated? Those who can, may, for all I care, and no doubt will, but I cannot. And the same kind of reasoning applies to Aubrey's story (1681) that when Sir William D'Avenant was in his cups, he liked to suggest, or to accept the suggestion, that he was Shakespeare's natural son (instead of his godson, as he may well have been). Mistress Davenant bore an unblemished reputation in her own time, and the gossip referred to began too late to be worth much, even if we are disposed to accept the authority of a drunken man giving countenance to a story "in which his mother had a very light report, whereby she was called a whore."

I have so far said nothing about that colossal literary bore, the "Dark Lady." "More folly has been written about the sonnets," says Chambers, "than about any other Shakespearean topic." About any literary topic whatever, I should say, except the apocalyptic books of the Bible.

Shakespeare's interest in dark beauty is not peculiar to the Sonnets; it occurs both in the early *Love's Labour's Lost* and the late *Antony and Cleopatra*. The real Cleopatra was pure Greek, but Shakespeare makes her as dark as W. W. Story did in the famous statue which Hawthorne described in *The Marble Faun*.

Whether the Dark Lady had an original or not does not seem to me a more promising or necessary subject for speculation than it would be with any other Shakespearean character. Nobody whose opinion matters doubts that there is a very large conventional element in the Sonnets, and when the Lady's swains ask me why, if they are wholly conventional, they make so much stronger an impression upon us than the other Elizabethan sonnet sequences, I can only reply that they were written by one William Shakespeare whose plays also make a stronger impression upon us than those written by other people. When Julia Marlowe was

asked whether it was necessary for an actress to have "lived" in order to act with power, she replied dryly, "One may enact Lady Macbeth convincingly without having first committed a murder." Exactly. Neither do I suppose Shakespeare to have strangled Anne Hathaway in their second best bed before writing *Othello* or to have been turned out into the storm by Susanna and Judith before *King Lear*. "In writing *The Cenci*," said Shelley, "my object was to see how I could succeed in describing passions I have never felt, and to tell the most dreadful story in pure and refined language. . . . *The Cenci* is a work of art, it is not colored by my feelings." An extreme statement, no doubt, and a great many writers do not function that way. I do not believe that Shakespeare did consistently, nor Shelley either. But in dealing with so objective a writer and one so free from egotism as I think Shakespeare was, Shelley's suggestion seems to me worthy of some consideration. "With this key Shakespeare unlocked his heart," wrote Wordsworth of the Sonnets. But Browning's reply was not impertinent. "If so, the less Shakespeare he."[32]

It is easy to make fun of Hazlitt for saying that he could make neither head nor tail of the ultimate drift of the Sonnets, but who has ever done so to the satisfaction of anybody except himself? The inability of the commentators to agree on any identification of the Friend, the Dark Lady, or the Rival Poet, to say nothing of whether Mr. W. H. was the Friend or merely the person who secured the copy for Thomas Thorpe's presumably unauthorized publication of 1609—all this has come perilously close to reducing the whole sonnet controversy to farce.

The champions of Southampton and Pembroke have been at each other's throats so long that memory runneth not to the contrary, but so far there has been no sign that either party will down

---

[32] C. J. Sisson, "The Mythical Sorrows of Shakespeare," *Proceedings of the British Academy*, 1934, makes fun of those who see all the emotions expressed in Shakespeare's plays determined by his personal experiences. "It appears that in 1607 Shakespeare's brother Edmund died, an event which helped to infuriate him. Fortunately, in 1608 his mother died, an event which restored him to a kindlier mood. So various are the effects of deaths in the family upon a great poet. The birth of a granddaughter helped, of course."

the other. Not so long ago, Leslie Hotson cried a plague on both their houses, introducing his own candidate, William Hatcliffe, but his methods resembled nothing so much as the cipher-hunting of the Baconians, and his most illustrious convert seems to have been himself.[33] We have not got it settled whether "Dark Lady" means a dark-complexioned Caucasian or a member of one of the dark-skinned races, and Peter Quennell even says that she is "an evil spirit, an occasion of offence, but [one who] scarcely takes shape as a human personage." In 1909 Frank Harris made Shakespeare's passion for Mary Fitton into one of the great pieces of literary mythology in this century;[34] later it appeared that if Shakespeare loved Mary Fitton, he may well have been one of the gentlemen who prefer blondes. G. B. Harrison was, I believe, the first to suggest "Lucy Negro" as the Dark Lady, and this suggestion was accepted by Fripp. More recently it was also taken up by Hotson, who does not, however, regard the woman as an African but sees "Negro" as a nickname and "black" as meaning proud or lusty. Her real name was Lucy Morgan, and she was one of the Queen's gentlewomen between 1579 and 1581. Going from bad to worse, she later lived in the stews, served a term in the Bridewell, and may have died of a venereal disease. Clearly there was such a person in Elizabethan England. But that she had any connection with Shakespeare Hotson does not succeed in showing at all.

At the risk of repeating myself, I must here say again that we are not discussing whether or not Shakespeare was capable of being enthralled by a Dark Lady—or a light one either. The question is plainly and simply one of evidence—or, rather, of the lack thereof. Personally I could much more easily conceive of his possible fall and enthrallment than I could of a man of his temperament writing what we now call "confessional" poetry, even in "sugared sonnets among his private friends." We may grant that there are sonnets which show a strong revulsion against sexual corruption,

---

[33] *Mr. W. H.* (Knopf, 1964).

[34] "Shakespeare's passion for Mary Fitton led him to shame and madness and despair; his strength broke down under the strain and he never won back again to health"—*The Man Shakespeare and his Tragic Life-Story* (Mitchell Kennerly, 1909).

and the same thing may be found in *Lear* and *Timon*. But Shakespeare had surely *seen* enough in his theater and his London to account for that without any more personal experience of corruption than we must all have from the mere circumstance of being human. Even the gentle Walter de la Mare, reading the news of "massacre, murder, filth, disgrace" in wartime, could conclude his meditation with

> "*Everything* human we comprehend,
> Only too well, too well!"

One other aspect of human conduct with moral implications has considerably interested the critics of Shakespeare, and this is his treatment of alcohol as a beverage.[35] He lived in a wine- and ale-drinking age (most modern beverages, both alcoholic and non-alcoholic being still in the future), but drinking as an element in hospitality is not often thrust into the foreground, except in some of the late plays, notably *Antony and Cleopatra*.[36] This background suits Antony, the only heavy drinker and reveler in "gaudy" nights among Shakespeare's heroes; Antony even dies with a drink:

> I am dying, Egypt, dying.
> Give me some wine and let me speak a little.

Cleopatra is a good match for him: she boasts of having drunk him "to his bed" by nine o'clock in the morning, and her maid Charmian seems to have shared her tastes in potations. Macbeth and his lady fortify themselves with wine before the murder of Duncan. Falstaff says Mrs. Page shares his fondness for sack, but we never see her drink it, and he is probably no more accurate here than in his other information about her. The old Shepherd in *The Winter's Tale* affectionately recalls his late wife at festival time,

[35] See Tolman, "Drunkenness in Shakespeare's Plays," *Falstaff and Other Shakespearean Topics*.

[36] The triumvirs' drinking scene (*Antony and Cleopatra*, II, 7), the most elaborate such in Shakespeare, is used to bring out the differences between their characters, but, according to his own statement in I, 4:16ff., even Octavius is far from strict about either drink or sex.

her face o' fire
With labour; and the thing she took to quench it,

but she of course, though a good woman, was not a "lady." There is more about men but not much more. Benedick promises not to lose more blood over the sorrows of love than he can get again with drinking, but nothing is made of this. Hamlet accuses Claudius of being a drunkard and even pretends to think him drunk after the play scene, but we never see Claudius under the influence, and the least we can say for him is that if Shakespeare did intend us to feel that this element was present, he certainly did not wish to emphasize it.

Excessive drinking is almost everywhere condemned. The worst drunkards in Shakespeare are Falstaff and his cronies, Sir Toby Belch, the villain Barnardine in *Measure for Measure* (who is hardly more than half human), and Cloten of *Cymbeline*, who is the perfect Elizabethan "roaring boy." The low-life characters in *The Tempest* are much addicted to alcohol, and Caliban takes to it with alacrity on first contact, as savages often do (Shakespeare seems to have known that too without anybody's telling him).[37]

As an element in his incomparable humor, Falstaff's indulgences may seem sometimes to be viewed leniently, but Falstaff is far from being entirely a comic character. The product of blended traditions, he is, as Baskervill used to point out, a braggart soldier, a professional rogue, and an alehouse jester, and in his most realistic aspect, he is a degenerate knight and gentleman who cannot rise. If the beginning of his break with Prince Hal is to be located at any specific point, it must be at Shrewsbury when he offers the Prince a bottle of sack for a pistol. Sir Toby, a junior cadet in Falstaff's company, presents his own less serious problems. Olivia disapproves of his drinking, and so does her steward Malvolio, but are we intended to sympathize with Malvolio or Sir Toby in the scene where the steward breaks in upon the revelers? The question is not an easy one. Malvolio is doing his duty, but he

---

[37] Another savage custom, that of smoking tobacco, which the explorers brought into England from the American Indians, Shakespeare never refers to; probably his keen sensitiveness to obnoxious odors protected him here.

is doing it in an egregious, self-righteous fashion, for he is an egregious, self-righteous man, and Toby flings at him the challenge which his descendants have been flinging at puritans ever since: "Dost thou think, because thou art virtuous, there shall be no more cakes and ale?" It may be that Shakespeare, in this instance, cried a plague upon both houses represented.[38]

Temperance in all things was a Renaissance ideal; Castiglione saw it as the foundation of all the virtues, with excess always offensive, and it is not surprising that the stock association of abstemiousness with hardness of heart, so prominent in later, popular drama (an important twentieth-century example would be Don Marquis' *The Old Soak*), should seem to occur only in connection with Prince John of Lancaster. Viola names drunkenness along with lying, babbling, and vainness as what she most dislikes, and Bassanio's Portia relishes the Saxon "sponge" least of all her unwelcome suitors ("when he is best, he is little worse than a man, and when he is worst, he is little better than a beast"). Hamlet expresses his contempt for Danish drinking, a custom, he thinks,

> More honour'd in the breach than the observance.
> This heavy-headed revel east and west
> Makes us traduc'd and tax'd of other nations.

And even the fool Slender, disillusioned in his drinking companions, vows never to get drunk again except with those who have the fear of God in them and not with drunken rogues.

Shakespeare's most effective temperance sermons, however, are

[38] Most readers are, I think, conscious of a somewhat similar division of sympathies in connection with the fall of Malvolio at the end of the play. Malvolio was perhaps E. H. Sothern's greatest role, and nobody who saw him in this scene will ever forget him. His was a comic-tragic creation of strength and power, but I cannot really believe that Shakespeare intended his audiences to take Malvolio's downfall quite so seriously as Sothern did, and if he had done so, I think they would have refused. Yet Olivia's "He hath been most notoriously abus'd," which is the last line spoken about Malvolio in the play, shows his creator to have realized that the steward had a case; he was always able to do that (Shylock is the star example), even when the plan of the play required the victim to be put down. See, in this connection, an ingenious article by Morris P. Tilley, "The Organic Unity of *Twelfth Night*," PMLA, XXIX (1914), 550–66, which sees the play as a glorification of the golden mean and classifies the characters as they approach or fail to approach this ideal.

put into the mouth of Cassio, after Iago, for his own purposes, has played upon his weak head to make him drunk: "O thou invisible spirit of wine, if thou hast no name to be known by, let us call thee devil!" and "O God, that men should put an enemy in their mouths to steal away their brains! That we should, with joy, pleasance, revel, and applause, transform ourselves into beasts!" Of course these are dramatic utterances, completely explicable in terms of the dramatic situation, but they are a very powerful statement of the antialcohol position, and in *As You Like It*, old Adam goes further still, attributing his health to his total abstinence from both alcohol and debauchery:

> Though I look old, yet I am strong and lusty;
> For in my youth I never did apply
> Hot and rebellious liquors in my blood,
> Nor did not with unbashful forehead woo
> The means of weakness and debility.

Tradition says that Adam was one of Shakespeare's roles; if so, then he wrote these lines for himself to speak. This does not prove anything, but it is not without interest. If his own known practice was notoriously out of line with Adam's, he might well have been inviting a laugh here which would not have been in his interest nor that of the play.

I have not of course forgotten the account of Shakespeare's death bequeathed to us by the Stratford vicar, John Ward: "Shakespeare, Drayton, and Ben Jonson had a merry meeting, and, it seems, drank too hard, for Shakespeare died of a fever there contracted." Why scholars who have been properly skeptical concerning the other slanders about Shakespeare should seem inclined to accept this is utterly beyond my comprehension. Ward did not even come to Stratford until 1662, forty-six years after Shakespeare's death, and when he arrived he was so ignorant of Shakespearean matters that he had not even read the plays. He "had heard" that Shakespeare was "a natural wit, without any art at all" and that he spent £1,000 a year, an incredible rate for his time. "Remember to peruse Shakespeare's plays," he tells him-

self, "and be versed in them, that I may not be ignorant in the matter." Even so, he does not himself vouch for what he has recorded: "it *seems*" that Shakespeare drank too hard and died of a fever. Is this the kind of language employed by a man who knows what he is talking about? and, incidentally, what kind of fatal fever is caused by drinking? Perhaps his ignorance of Shakespeare's plays was not what Ward ought to have worked on first. As Smart has pointed out, some of the other entries in his commonplace book inform us "that the Egyptians kept their wives at home by allowing them no shoes; that herring is a treacherous meat," and that Milton was a disguised Roman Catholic. And with that we may leave him.[39]

[39] For other references to Shakespeare's drinking, see Chambers II, 286–87, 291. But these are obviously even more of the legendary variety than the Ward story.

V

SOCIETY

I

There is no indication in Shakespeare's plays that he was ambitious to frame what could be called a social or political philosophy, but there are interesting suggestions here and there. I do not get the impression that he greatly admired political professionals. No doubt his frequent references to Julius Caesar indicate interest, yet his treatment of the great man in the play which bears his name is ambivalent. Such epithets as "this vile politician" and "a scurvy politician" who seems to see what is not there are not unfamiliar in his plays. The political type is gifted at ingratiating himself, but he makes no strong impression of sincerity. All too often, his success is encrusted with blood. Henry IV's whole reign was shadowed by fear of God's vengeance for Richard's dethronement and death, fribble though he had been, and his son tries to bribe God to overlook this sin before he goes into battle against the French. Even the saintly Henry VI asks,

> But, Clifford, tell me, didst thou never hear
> That things ill-got had ever bad success?

which recalls, by contrast, Macbeth's "things bad begun make strong themselves by ill." It was Macbeth's feeling that

I am in blood
Stepp'd in so far that, should I wade no more,
Returning were as tedious as go o'er.

As tedious, perhaps, but in the end more profitable. For him there is no strengthening his position through repeated outrage. That was not the way Shakespeare's moral world was built.[1]

England does not quite escape criticism in Shakespeare's plays; the First Gravedigger in *Hamlet* sounds very much like Shaw when he suggests that the mad Prince was sent to England because his madness would not be noticed there, all the men being as mad as he. Iago sees Shakespeare's countrymen as accomplished topers, and Trinculo wishes he could exhibit Caliban in England where any monster "makes" a man and every "holiday fool" would give a piece of silver to look at him. "When they will not give a doit to relieve a lame beggar, they will lay out ten to see a dead Indian." But all this kind of thing ranks as harmless fun beside such a magnificent passage as the dying Gaunt's eulogy of

This royal throne of kings, this sceptred isle,
This earth of majesty, this seat of Mars,

---

[1] Reference has been made elsewhere in this book to Iago as an example of that degenerate type of the artist temperament which finds satisfaction in manipulating actual, not created, characters. But in his use of human beings as things, or means toward an end rather than ends in themselves, he also suggests the politician. Thus he destroys Desdemona for his own purposes, quite without having anything against her personally; indeed he once asserts that he "loves" her! Tucker Brooke ("Shakespeare's Study in Culture and Anarchy") saw Shakespeare depicting the political factions of his own England in *Troilus and Cressida*—"the febrile Essex type of decadent chivalry" and "the strident go-getters of the newer dispensation: Cecil-Ulysses and Raleigh-Diomed." He "sensed in Thersites the lowering shadow of Prynne and the iconoclasts, foresaw in Pandarus the portrait of the scandalous Carr, Earl of Somerset." Could all this be established, it would also establish keen political interests, insights, and convictions on Shakespeare's part, but I fear it is highly conjectural, though I agree with Brooke when he argues, in another essay, that Shakespeare's patriotism was essentially old-fashioned, "that of the Tory country dwellers." Both papers are in Brooke's *Essays on Shakespeare and Other Elizabethans* (YUP, 1949).

This other Eden, demi-paradise,[2]

and Mowbray's woeful expression of his passion for the English language, when Richard II banishes him, is almost as effective (since Shakespeare was a writer, it may even have lain closer to his own heart):

> The language I have learn'd these forty years,
> My native English, now I must forgo;
> And now my tongue's use is to me no more
> Than an unstringed viol or a harp,
> Or like a cunning instrument cas'd up,
> Or, being open, put into his hands
> That knows no touch or tune of harmony.

Foreign affectations are satirized from time to time in Shakespeare's plays; Rosalind, for one, takes up a rather contemptuous attitude toward travelers as men who have sold their own lands to view those of others and who therefore have seen much but have nothing. In *Romeo and Juliet* there are suggestions that the duel is un-English. To be sure, there are hints of the inferiority complex here and there. In *Richard II*, York calls the English a "tardy, apish nation" for imitating Italian manners, and Richard III speaks of "French nods and apish courtesy." *Henry V*, however, is full of expressions of contempt for the French, which is carried to a ridiculous extreme in the roll call of the dead after Agincourt, which shows that the French have lost 10,000 men and the English only twenty-five, of whom but four were men of rank! The King's difficulties with the French language in the wooing scene are of course quite unhistorical, for French had just ceased to be the official English court language.

---

[2] The Bastard's closing speech in *King John*, beginning

> This England never did, nor never shall,
> Lie at the proud foot of a conqueror,
> But when it first did help to wound itself,

is nearly as splendid as Gaunt's speech. The passage from *Richard II*, magnificently read by John Gielgud, was included in the phonograph record issued to commemorate the coronation of King George VI in 1937—HMV 24015–S.

The Duke of Albany fights against King Lear's party, even after breaking with his wife, because it is headed by the French monarchy, and he feels bound to repel the invader of British soil. Was Shakespeare unable to bring himself to depict the triumph of French arms on the English stage, even though it had occurred in the source play? It may be so, though one must admit that a happy ending to the play Shakespeare was writing would have been fantastic. But there are problems too in *Cymbeline*, where the King boasts that Britons are "a warlike people," as if that were praise. Why did the dramatist allow such evil characters as Cloten and the Queen to express such flaming ideals of British patriotism? And why in the name of common sense did Cymbeline voluntarily agree to pay the disputed tribute at the end of the play, after he had defeated the Romans, thus making the war itself utterly useless?

The famous passage in *A Midsummer Night's Dream* about "a fair vestal throned by the West," which has been referred to elsewhere, is generally, and I think rightly, taken as a compliment to Queen Elizabeth, and the glories of her reign are foretold at the end of *Henry VIII*. But Shakespeare contributed nothing to the outburst of commendatory writing which followed her death; indeed Chettle rebuked him for this. Shakespeare's company was in high favor with the new monarch, James I, and at one time the dramatist himself served as Groom of the Chamber,[3] but this was purely a formal matter. It would seem that the King must have been much on Shakespeare's mind when he wrote *Macbeth*, not only because he was implicationally involved in the vision of the future which the witches project in Act IV, Scene 2, but also because a number of James's interests appear prominently in the drama. In 1605, when James visited Oxford, he was entertained by a pageant in which three weird sisters appeared before him, reminding him that in former days they had appeared to Banquo, and prophesying his future greatness.

There is a story about a (let us hope) prescient little girl who, having watched a parade of soldiers, remarked, "You know what I

[3] See Adams, *Life*, 365–72.

think? Someday they will give a war, and nobody will come." This almost happened in London on Sunday morning, February 8, 1601, when the Essex conspirators, among whom the Earl of Southampton was prominent, raised the banner of rebellion in the streets and the citizens prudently stayed indoors. The afternoon before a revival of Shakespeare's *Richard II* had been arranged at the Globe, apparently with the naïve idea in mind that having seen a king deposed and murdered on the stage on Saturday afternoon, Londoners would be ready to depose and perhaps murder a queen in earnest on Sunday morning. Elizabeth did not miss the point; she well knew that she had often been compared to Richard II.[4] Was the deposition scene itself performed on this occasion? The usual view seems to be that it was generally omitted (it was not printed in 1597). If it was given, one marvels that the actors escaped so lightly; they were interrogated but promptly cleared of blame. If, on the other hand, it was not, how could even a mind like that of Essex have staked so much upon this performance? Before February had run out, he had lost his head; Southampton was imprisoned for the rest of the Queen's lifetime, and there are those who think that Shakespeare held this against her. But there is no evidence that he and Southampton were in any way associated at this time nor that he had placed his chips upon the unreliable Essex either. Certainly one would hate to think so. If he did, what became of his belief in "order"? As for his silence at Elizabeth's death, he simply did not write occasional verses.

II

The Shakespeares were not aristocrats, but the family did have modest aristocratic connections, though more on the mother's than the father's side. Does an aristocratic bias show in the omission of all mention of Magna Charta from *King John*? In *All's Well* the King of France admires the aristocratic bearing of Bertram's late father:

---

[4] See Lily B. Campbell's cogent discussion of this matter in *Shakespeare's "Histories,"* especially pp. 171–212, and cf. her statement of purpose, p. 6.

> Who were below him
> He us'd as creatures of another place,
> And bow'd his eminent top to their low ranks,
> Making them proud of his humility,
> In their poor praise he humbled.

But when Bertram objects to wedding Helena because of her inferior station, the King at once declares that he "can build up" that matter very easily by granting her a title:

> Strange is it that our bloods,
> Of colour, weight, and heat, pour'd all together,
> Would quite confound distinction, yet [stand] off
> In differences so mighty.

It was to take the world a long time to find out that there is no white nor black nor any other kind of blood, and that the Bible is quite accurate when it declares that God has made of one blood all the nations of the earth, and even yet the world knows this only scientifically, not emotionally. Yet, in the popular sense of the term, "blood tells" in Guiderius and Arviragus, who have been brought up in the wilderness, and with Perdita, who has lived in a shepherd's cottage; these are cultivated people worthy to inhabit any court, and Professor Tolman used to be fond of saying of Perdita that in her case not only does blood tell but it tells her everything other people must learn by hard study. Probably, however, this does not mean anything more than that Shakespeare wished to give suitable style and gentility to serious, praiseworthy characters.

Sonnet 66 shows that Shakespeare was well aware of corruptions in the body politic, and Hamlet speaks bitterly of

> The oppressor's wrong, the [proud] man's contumely,
> The pangs of dispriz'd love, the law's delay,
> The insolence of office, and the spurns
> That patient merit of the unworthy takes.

Such passages justify Masson's comment that "society . . . did not

seem to Shakespeare all right, but in many things sadly out of joint."

The First Fisherman in *Pericles* is convinced that the fish in the sea behave much like men on land:

> the great ones eat up the little ones. I can compare our rich misers to nothing so fitly as to a whale, 'a plays and tumbles, driving the poor fry before him, and at last devour them all at a mouthful. Such whales have I heard on o' the land, who never leave gaping till they swallow'd the whole parish, church, steeple, bells, and all.

But the best utterances of social criticism in the canonical plays are given to King Lear:

> Thou rascal beadle, hold thy bloody hand!
> Why dost thou lash that whore? Strip thy own back;
> Thou hotly lusts to use her in that kind
> For which thou whip'st her. The usurer hangs the cozener.
> Through tatter'd clothes great vices do appear;
> Robes and furr'd gowns hide all,

and, better still:

> Poor naked wretches, wheresoe'er you are,
> That bide the pelting of this pitiless storm,
> How shall your houseless heads and unfed sides,
> Your loop'd and window'd raggedness, defend you,
> From seasons such as these? O, I have ta'en
> Too little care of this! Take physic pomp;
> Expose thyself to feel what wretches feel,
> That thou mayst shake the superflux to them,
> And show the heavens more just.[5]

Temperamentally, however, Shakespeare was no reformer, and we can hardly find him advocating specific reforms without con-

---

[5] Gloucester, too, becomes more sensitive to the sufferings of the poor through what he himself experiences, and there is a good deal of social consciousness in that part of the play of *Sir Thomas More* which some scholars believe Shakespeare wrote.

siderable straining. Perhaps it is the passages which throw out suggestions but do not actually commit him to anything which are the most interesting. When in *The Merchant of Venice* Bassanio begs to be allowed to proceed to his choice of the caskets on the ground that "as I am, I live upon the rack," Portia playfully scents treason in his love. There is none, he says, but the "ugly treason of mistrust," and Portia replies,

> Ay, but I fear you speak upon the rack,
> Where men enforced do speak anything.

If this is true, then of course torture is useless in investigating the truth of an accusation. Joan of Arc had understood that long before Shakespeare when she told her judges that if they put her on the rack, she would say anything they wished her to say to stop the pain, but that since she would take it all back afterwards, they would have gained nothing. We have been told that Shakespeare, through Portia's "subversive" suggestion, is here making a very early covert protest against the use of torture in judicial procedure. But though I cannot conceive of Shakespeare wishing to torture anybody, this seems to me to place a heavier weight upon the passage under consideration than it can comfortably bear. In the court scene in the same play, Shylock justifies his insistence upon his bond on the ground that the treatment which the Venetians mete out to their slaves, asses, dogs, and mules disqualifies them from judging him adversely.

> The pound of flesh, which I demand of him,
> Is dearly bought; 'tis mine and I will have it.

The point is a good one, but I find in it no covert or explicit condemnation of slavery on Shylock's part. The question of capital punishment is more interesting. I should not go so far as to say that Shakespeare was opposed to it, but the hangman's office is not a dignified one in his pages. Imogen thinks it about what Cloten is fit for, and Prince Hal teases Falstaff by first suggesting that, after he becomes king, he will make him a judge and then cruelly dashes his hopes by indicating that he will only employ him as a hang-

man. And in *Measure for Measure* the hangman's office is likened to that of a bawd. "Go to, sir," says the Provost, "you weigh equally. A feather will turn the scale." On the other hand, I am willing to grant that the presence of English, Scottish, Welsh, and Irish soldiers in Henry V's army *may* indicate some interest in the idea of a united Britain on Shakespeare's part, and *The Tempest* suggests that he did know that the new world was being colonized and that the colonizers were not always above reproach in their treatment of the natives. It would not be difficult for me to argue that the discussion of good old Gonzalo's utopian ideas in Act II, Scene 1 reflects Shakespeare's own common sense, and if I were to set out to make my own allegory of *The Tempest*, having rejected all the allegories which others have discovered in it, it would be that Prospero represents the man of the future, who, if humanity is to survive, must combine power with wisdom and good will. Nor would it have been a bad idea to have had embossed and hung up over the desks of several recent presidents of the United States the words of King John:

> O, where hath our intelligence been drunk?
> Where hath it slept?

III

But what, now, of the social problems that concern us most? Did Shakespeare take up any attitude toward racial and/or religious prejudice?

In the modern sense, no, for modern problems did not exist in his time, but the racial question is at least suggested in connection with both his "Moors" (who were, in his mind, as his descriptions of them show, indistinguishable from Negroes). Aaron in *Titus Andronicus* is more devil than man, and if we had this example alone, we might see Shakespeare sunk deep in the quagmires of prejudice, but Othello is as noble as Aaron is base. Shakespeare uses Othello's racial difference for picturesqueness, to make his yielding to overwhelming passion more believable (the North has always considered Southern peoples passionate), and, above all, to

give Iago a better chance to convince him that, being a foreigner, he does not understand the ways of Italian women and may therefore easily have been deceived by one of them. Whatever the reader may believe about interracial marriage, to see the love of Othello and Desdemona as merely sensual or degrading is to accept Iago's, not Shakespeare's, interpretation of it; on her part, at least, quite the opposite was the case, as her creator takes pains to have her inform us:

> I saw Othello's visage in his mind,
> And to his honours and his valiant parts
> Did I my soul and fortunes consecrate.[6]

Though there are several derogatory references to Jews elsewhere in Shakespeare, the question of the writer's attitude (if he had one) becomes important only in *The Merchant of Venice*, a play which has occasioned extraordinary difference of opinion. The prejudice here is religious, not racial; nobody except the girl's father seems to disapprove of the Jessica-Lorenzo marriage. It is clear of course that Shylock is the villain of the play (he plots murder) and that its design requires him to be put down. It is true also that his Jewishness is insisted upon again and again. Nevertheless Shakespeare does give him a point of view and shows clearly that he himself understands it. I cannot deny that upon the whole we are intended to admire Antonio nor that Shakespeare does not anywhere tell us that he disapproves of what has been called Antonio's "expectatory method" of manifesting his dislike for Jews, but surely the Elizabethans were not all such savages that they needed to have this spelled out. Shylock *is* wronged by his daughter; he *is* humanized by his reference to his dead wife; the

---

[6] Portia takes up a different attitude toward the Prince of Morocco ("Let all of his complexion choose me so"), but he is still presented more favorably than Arragon. One gifted female adherent of the school of criticism which holds that a work of art is what we can read into it, wrote: "In studying the play of *Othello*, I have always imagined the hero a *white* man. It is true the dramatist paints him black, but this shade does not suit the man. It is a stage decoration, which my taste discards; a fault of colour from the artistic point of view." Furness quotes this in his edition of the play, then comments slyly, "The Authoress dates her Preface from 'Oaklands, Harford County, Maryland.'"

austerity of his life *does* inspire respect, no matter how much one may disagree with him; his indictment of those who despise him merely because he is a Jew is unanswerable, and Shakespeare has the wit to permit none of his enemies to attempt an answer. Compared to Marlowe's Jew, Shylock is a man standing over against a monster. A distinguished scholar has discounted all this on the ground that Shakespeare always humanizes his villains. Does he? Iago? Aaron? Cloten? Don John? Borachio? Cornwall? Goneril and Regan?

It is not easy to be completely fair about this matter at the present time, and the enforced conversion at the end makes it all the more difficult. Jessica converts voluntarily, but it is hard not to agree with Launcelot that the principal effect of this spiritual achievement will be to raise the price of pork. I am not saying that this would be the Elizabethan attitude, yet the fact remains that an Elizabethan dramatist *did* express the idea through an Elizabethan character. Lorenzo believed that Shylock's only chance of salvation was "for his gentle daughter's sake," but Lorenzo was not a theologian. No doubt many Elizabethans believed that Jessica had achieved salvation through converting, and some of them may have believed the same thing about Shylock. But Reformation theologians were far more sophisticated than moderns often give them credit for being. Luther did not believe baptism necessary to salvation; neither did Calvin nor Hooker.[7] Shylock *does* escape the death penalty he had incurred, and though he loses dignity with us when he saves his life by changing his religion, the Elizabethans probably considered that he had little to lose.

Caroline Spurgeon's study of Shakespeare's imagery left her with the feeling that Shakespeare was strongly antiwar. Nobody would rather believe this than I; surely one of the most creative spirits who ever lived ought to have been consistently hostile to the great destroyer. Unfortunately, however, I can find little real evidence to support this view.

[7] See Roland Mushat Frye, *Shakespeare and Christian Doctrine* (Princeton University Press, 1963), 20–22.

There are, to be sure, antiwar passages in Shakespeare, and I certainly do not mean to suggest that Shakespeare was a war lover. Young Henry VI thinks it a scandal that Christians should fight one another, but perhaps there are not enough of them to count.[8] It is frankly recognized that war means ruinous taxation,[9] rape, and the slaughter of prisoners, old men, and infants; Henry V disclaims responsibility for these evils if his demands are not met, though he will have no pillaging. We are probably intended to be horrified by the scene in 3 *Henry VI* (II, 5) showing a son who has killed his father in battle and a father who has killed his son. In *Measure for Measure* doubt is expressed of the truly pacific intentions of any military man, and Boult in *Pericles* complains that a man "may serve seven years for the loss of a leg, and have not money enough in the end to buy him a wooden one." I cannot believe that Shakespeare was cynical enough to approve of Henry IV's advice to his son,

> Be it thy course to busy giddy minds
> With foreign quarrels,

though this advice has certainly been followed by half the chancelleries of the world. How much Henry IV cares for peace may be inferred from his eagerness to have the English wars ended so that he may rush off to the Holy Land and fight there, and even in *Hamlet* "old Fortinbras," suppressing the proposed expedition of his nephew against the Danes, forthwith authorizes an attack upon the Poles to make use of the matériel! In *King John* (II, 1), Chatillon brilliantly describes the "unsettled humours of the

---

8 "The sixteenth century saw the development of a crisis in the conflict between the authority of the church and that of the state, between Catholics and Reformers, and between sect and sect. Fundamental problems arose to be argued: whether a Christian state might make war, whether it might war on another Christian state, and whether it might make war for religion's sake"—Lily B. Campbell, *Shakespeare's "Histories"* . . . , 264.

9 Northumberland reproaches Richard II for having spent lavishly in peace time,

> for warr'd he hath not,
> But basely yielded upon compromise
> That which his noble ancestors achiev'd with blows.

He seems to think that bankruptcy via the war route would have been nobler.

land" that flock to the standard to make "a hazard of new fortunes" whenever such an expedition is toward.

Romeo and Juliet is very pacific so far as private war is concerned, and the dramatist's attitude toward the feud is consistently hostile.[10] I do not recall ever to have seen it pointed out that when Romeo is challenged by Tybalt, his new-found love for Juliet inspires him to do a bit of creative independent thinking. For the moment at least, he rejects the "gentlemanly" code on which he has been brought up to try out the method of non-resistance, and if he had been left to his own devices, this might well have worked.

Actually, the character who has the most rational attitude toward war is Falstaff. Everything he says about "honor" in his famous soliloquy at Shrewsbury is true,[11] but nobody in his senses would argue that Shakespeare intended us to accept Sir John as the spokesman for a progressive or advanced moral viewpoint. Falstaff's rationalism is only a mock-rationalism, inspired by his own selfishness and laziness, and what he says serves more an aesthetic than a moral purpose, being intended as a kind of comic counterpoint to the very different and more "noble" ideas expressed by the serious characters of the play. This kind of counterpoint is not unusual in Shakespeare; further examples occur in *The Two Gentlemen of Verona*, *A Midsummer Night's Dream*, *As You Like It*, and other plays.

With *Troilus and Cressida* the situation is different. This is the play which gives us the priceless description of man as warrior—"Mars his idiot"—and in which war and lechery confounds all. Though Troilus is called "the prince of chivalry" (antedating that ideal by many centuries), nothing about either chivalry or the military virtues is treated respectfully. The war for a rotten cause was not worth fighting, and at the end it is left hanging in the air.

[10] G. B. Harrison, *Shakespeare Under Elizabeth* (Holt, 1933), 73–75, does not succeed in showing that *Romeo and Juliet* was suggested by a feud between the Danvers family and the Longs, but his discussion does show that such matters in real life were not unfamiliar to Shakespeare's audiences.

[11] See too his misuse of the king's press, especially in 1 *Henry IV* (IV, 2) and 2 *Henry IV* (III, 2). If the military draft rejected all the really fit men, as Falstaff does, it would be much less harmful to society.

Achilles was always one of the most detestable characters in literature, but surely he is nowhere else quite so contemptible as in this
play, and though Hector is more respectworthy, even he is betrayed by his adherence (in Act II, Scene 2) to the useless superstition of saving face.

Renaissance courtesy writers solemnly debated whether prowess
in arms was superior or inferior to learning. Castiglione gave the
palm to arms; Guazzo decided that "of all the things we possess
in the world, learning only is durable and immortal." Both, however, take soldiership for granted as a normal part of man's experience, and so, I think, does Shakespeare, in Jaques' Seven Ages
of Man speech and elsewhere.[12] All the gentlemen in *Much Ado*
are valiant soldiers, and though quarrelsomeness in private life
seems to be condemned, Beatrice has no hesitation in asking
Benedick to kill Claudio after the latter's repudiation of Hero. It is
part of the nobility of Cymbeline's sons that they should be
thrilled by tales of valor long before they have been exposed to
fighting, and that wild horses could not hold them back from
rushing off to battle at the first opportunity offered.

> What thing is it that I never
> Did see man die, scarce ever looked on blood,
> But that of coward hares, hot goats, and venison!

(The voice of "Mars his idiot" indeed!) The Duke in *Measure for
Measure* is "a scholar, a statesman, and a soldier," and, as has
already been noted, Ophelia laments the overthrow in Hamlet of
"the courtier's, soldier's, scholar's eye, tongue, sword."[13] The

[12] The usual view is that Shakespeare himself saw no military service, the
principal argument to the contrary being that of Duff Cooper, *Sergeant Shakespeare*
(VP, 1950), where he is seen as having enlisted under Leicester for service in the
Netherlands. Though the work of a military man, this rather charming little book is
not militaristic in spirit. Duff Cooper has not "proved" anything, but he handles
his evidence quite as responsibly as most professional Shakespeare scholars do. He
does not try to make a military hero out of Shakespeare. "It is possible that, having
scented the battlefield, he found, as soldiers often have done, the air of the
metropolis more congenial." The book is written in the form of a letter to the
author's wife, Lady Diana Cooper, and at the end he asks her, "Have I convinced
you? I have almost convinced myself."

[13] Are we intended to admire Fortinbras in this play? The dramatist's attitude

"pride, pomp, and circumstance of glorious war" fascinates Desdemona in Othello, though pacifists may perhaps console themselves with the thought that the villainous Iago is also a professional military man, and they might even make a point of the fact that Othello, noble as he is, kills his wife. For that matter, Aufidius, who welcomes Coriolanus as his ally and then turns against him and has him murdered, for no reason but that he believes him to be more highly regarded than himself by the Volscians, is almost as unscrupulous.

Coriolanus and *Henry V* are the most military plays. Coriolanus and his bloodthirsty mother not only accept war but positively revel in it, wounds and all, and Valeria even admires violence in Coriolanus' child as a promise that he will grow up to resemble his father.[14] It is true that the mother Volumnia partially redeems herself in the course of the play, when she successfully pleads with her son to save Rome, thus proving that she really does put her country ahead of her personal desires, which is more than can be said for him, for he joins forces with Rome's enemies out of personal pique, and it may be that Shakespeare was here dramatizing woman's stronger inclination to accept the "best possible." What Volumnia says for peace in the scene of intercession is about all anybody says for it in the course of the play however. Incidentally, we never learn what the Romans and the Volscians were fighting about, and the war seems to stop and start again in obedience to quite private whims and motives.

Critics like Bradley, Sir Arthur Quiller-Couch, and John Masefield have frankly hated Henry V, and sometimes such writers try to persuade us that Shakespeare did not admire him either but merely tried to create a popular hero for popular consumption. I

---

seems to me somewhat ambivalent. The soliloquy in Act IV, Scene 4 would appear to contrast two opposite extremes—the man who fights foolishly, for nothing, and the man who will not fight even with an adequate cause. Yet Hamlet gets a military funeral, and Fortinbras is dignified and anything but irresponsible in the one scene in which he actually appears, at the end of the play.

[14] A woman of a gentler, and more Shakespearean, sort is the wife of Coriolanus, Virgilia, and Shakespeare must have had some interest in her, for he makes her a considerably more developed character than she was in his source.

share the outlook of such writers, but I find no evidence to support their conclusion. Perhaps because it harmonizes with his own conception of Shakespeare as an "entrancing, brilliant mossback," completely unmoved by the expansionist spirit of his time, Tucker Brooke[15] saw Henry as having "prudential and legalistic aims in invading France, but no imperial aims." But this does not get us very far. The play *Henry V* glorifies all the military virtues, in the great battle speech in Act III, Scene 1, for example (though here too Bardolph is allowed his comic counterpoint immediately afterward), and if it does not mean what it says, then it means nothing. What is interesting in *Henry V* is the long discussion in Act IV, Scene 1, concerning the soldier's personal responsibility, or the lack of it, in an unjust war. The King's point of view is that though the king is responsible to God, his subjects are responsible only to him; if the cause be unjust, God will punish the king but hold the soldier who merely obeyed his orders free of blame. I do not know—nor greatly care—what Shakespeare "believed" about all this; the interesting matter is the discussion. Something like it comes up again in the course of the plays whenever a ruler or a nobleman orders somebody put to death, and it is notable that those who have received such commissions often evade them. In *Richard III* the First Murderer of the Duke of Clarence asks the Second whether he is afraid to kill him. "Not to kill him," he replies, "having a warrant; but to be damn'd for killing him, from the which no warrant can defend me." This utterance seems quite at home in the individualistic, highly Protestant world in which Puritanism rose to power, for it is the essence of Puritanism that every man is directly responsible to God for his own soul and that that responsibility cannot be shoved off upon any other individual or any institution. The world has been incredibly and stupidly slow in perceiving the application of all this to war, but the application is being made today, and this of course is why Renaissance preconsiderations of the matter now interest us.

[15] *Shakespeare of Stratford* (YUP, 1926), especially pp. 146, 148, 150, 154. See also in this volume "The Personality of Shakespeare," pp. 136–60.

IV

If Shakespeare had any one strong political conviction, it was that of the importance of order in the body politic. This was common to many Elizabethans, for the horrors of the War of the Roses were still vividly kept in mind and imagination, and no doubt this was one of the reasons why so many Elizabethans welcomed the Tudor peace even though they had to accept the Tudor tyranny along with it. It was no accident that Shakespeare helped perpetuate the diabolical version of the still controversial character of Richard III, slain by the founder of the Tudor line at Bosworth Field.

The standard statement of Shakespeare's respect for order is in the great speech of Ulysses in *Troilus and Cressida* (I, 3)—"the specialty of rule hath been neglected"—where the problem is not pondered within the limited range where contemporary controversialists generally chose to place it, but philosophically grounded in the nature of creation itself.[16] This is by all means the greatest speech in the play and one of the memorable display pieces in Shakespeare; only the unpopularity and comparative unfamiliarity of the play in which it occurs has kept it from being more famous than it is.

It does not, however, stand alone. Instead, the basic idea occurs again and again in so many connections as to suggest that it was a firmly rooted part of Shakespeare's thinking. In *The Comedy of Errors* the Duke of Ephesus seems even to commit himself to the thesis that man was made for law, not law for man, when he condemns old Egeus in spite of his sympathy for him, and Theseus takes up the same attitude toward Hermia, though in both these cases the law is considerately overlooked in the end out of regard for a happy ending to the comedy. Adriana, in *Errors*, applies the order principle to marriage, as does Katherine the Shrew after her conversion. The Duke in *Measure for Measure* believes in law enforcement, though admitting his own laxity in this regard, and the Prince of Verona is convinced that "mercy but murders, par-

[16] For further comment upon the religious implications of this matter, see Frye, 195–99.

doning those that kill." The bitter irony of Timon in his terrible pagan prayer (*Timon of Athens*, IV, 1) also stresses the importance of order. The basic reason for the rejection of Falstaff is no doubt his general moral worthlessness and bad influence, but it is probably not without significance that his fall comes immediately after he has outraged all royal decorum by breaking in upon Hal's formal train on their way to the Abbey.

Professor Harbage has called attention to the speeches of the Archbishop of Canterbury in *Henry V* (I, 2:183–212) and of Menenius in *Coriolanus* (I, 1:99–109, 132–45); like that of Ulysses, he points out, each is "delivered by an unscrupulous politician meeting an immediate problem—advocating a practical program of somewhat debatable merit." Shakespeare knew, and elsewhere tells us, that "the devil can cite Scripture for his purpose," but I believe he also knew that this does not invalidate the Scripture itself. In *Hamlet* (IV, 5), even the usurper Claudius eloquently asserts both the principle of order and the "divinity [that] doth hedge a king" in language which partakes of blasphemy in the mouth of one who has himself murdered his king and kept the throne away from the king's son. Nevertheless his theory is sound, his fault being merely that his practice has not squared with it.

VI

THE ANGEL OF THE WORLD

I

Many persons appear to believe that Shakespeare was emphatically a man of this world, that he showed little interest in religion, and that his religious references are few and insignificant. Though nothing could be more ridiculous than to try to make him appear a devotee (certainly he had nothing like Milton's interest in religion, nor even, I believe, Chaucer's), his text abounds with references to the Bible[1] and to Christian doctrines, practices, and institutions, often even in plays set in pagan

[1] For a full study of Shakespeare's Biblical references, the reader must turn to William Burgess, *The Bible in Shakespeare: A Study of the Relation of the Works of William Shakespeare to the Bible* . . . (Crowell, 1903) and to Raymond Noble, *Shakespeare's Biblical Knowledge and Use of the Book of Common Prayer* (M, 1935). My own Biblical references were gathered together before I had examined these books, and my religious chapter first written before I had read Roland Mushat Frye, *Shakespeare and Christian Doctrine*, and Robert H. West, *Shakespeare and the Outer Mystery* (University of Kentucky Press, 1968). Nevertheless I have derived much stimulation and encouragement from both Frye and West, to whom not only I but Shakespearean scholarship in general must stand indebted. Frye's knowledge of Reformation theology proves unexpectedly illuminative of Shakespeare; see, for example, in his introduction, the discussion of why Shakespeare's emphasis upon "secular, temporal, non-theological" concerns was exactly what "the major theologians influencing England in the sixteenth century would have expected from literature."

times. "O, for my beads!" cries Dromio of Syracuse, "I cross me for a sinner." *Pericles* contains a reference to "the whole parish, church, steeple, bells and all." Religion "groans" at the ingratitude of Timon's false friends. We have a "state of grace" in *Troilus and Cressida*, a "century of prayers," orisons, and "election" in *Cymbeline*. Theseus gives Hermia a forbidding report on convent life. Saturninus in *Titus Andronicus* mixes up "priest and holy water" with swearing by the Roman gods, and the Clown speaks of his inability to say grace. Even Aaron, "an irreligious Moor," seems to entertain the Christian conception of hell at least as an hypothesis, and in *King Lear* both the monarch and his Fool babble of steeples and holy water in the storm scene. In the pagan *Rape of Lucrece* "the blackest sin is cleared with absolution." Othello has many Christian references; Imogen speaks much of the gods and of prayer.

The frame of reference against which the plays exist is, then, definitely Christian, and this the dramatist seems to take for granted for both his characters and his audience. Shakespeare makes King Henry IV refer to "all the kingdoms that acknowledge Christ," and there can be no doubt that he himself thought of England as one of them. If not many of his characters specifically call themselves Christians, as Desdemona does, the reason may well be that their creator thought such affirmation unnecessary. Richard II, always a master of words, speaks of

> the sepulchre in stubborn Jewry,
> Of the world's ransom, blessed Mary's Son,

and his great opponent, Henry IV, dreams persistently of organizing a crusade

> To chase these pagans in those holy fields
> Over whose acres walk'd those blessed feet
> Which fourteen hundred years ago were nail'd
> For our advantage on the bitter cross.

The dramatist stressed heavily the religious side of Henry V, making him considerably more pious than he had been in the

sources. He calls himself "a Christian king," and the Chorus adds, "the mirror of all Christian kings." "O God, thy arm was here," exclaims the monarch after his victory at Agincourt, and orders the singing of "Non nobis" and "Te deum." The twentieth century may well not find much more spiritual uplift here than in Mistress Quickly's comfortable conviction that all is in God's hands, but that is beside the point.

Launcelot in *The Merchant of Venice* speaks of Ash Wednesday, the Clown in *All's Well* of Shrove Tuesday, and Mrs. Overdone in *Measure for Measure* of "Philip and Jacob"—the day of St. Philip and St. James. Henry V fights on St. Crispin's Day, and St. Lambert's Day is selected for judicial combat in *Richard II*. Good Friday is spoken of in both *King John* and *Henry IV*, and perhaps the most beautiful religious passage in Shakespeare is this reference to Christmas in *Hamlet*:

> Some [say] that ever 'gainst that season comes
> Wherein our Saviour's birth is celebrated,
> The bird of dawning singeth all night long;
> And then, they say, no spirit can walk abroad;
> The nights are wholesome; then no planets strike,
> No fairy [takes], nor witch hath power to charm,
> So hallow'd and so gracious is the time.

There are few references to the Blessed Virgin, but Gonzalo in *The Tempest* once swears by her ("By'r lakin"), and the Princess in *Love's Labour's Lost* exclaims, "Our Lady help my lord!" Fasting for religious purposes is mentioned in *Henry IV* and *Measure for Measure*. Juliet goes to confession, and when Portia leaves for Venice, she pretends to be making a retreat near Belmont. Oliver in *As You Like It* speaks of his reformation as a "conversion," and the usurping Duke's change of heart is specifically ascribed to his meeting with "an old religious man."

As to the Bible specifically, Portia cites the Lord's Prayer in her appeal to Shylock, who could hardly have admitted its authority, and Shylock himself speaks of Jacob and Laban, calls Jesus a "Nazarite," meaning Nazarene, and seems to know something of

the New Testament when he refers in passing to the demoniac whose expelled demons were allowed to take refuge in a herd of swine. Gratiano, who hardly seems a religious type, avows his Christian faith in the court scene of *The Merchant of Venice*, having previously referred to the New Testament condemnation upon those who call their brothers fools.

Orlando refers to the parable of the Prodigal Son, and Judas, "that did betray the Best," is referred to in both *As You Like It* and *The Winter's Tale*. Golgotha is spoken of in *Richard II* and *Macbeth*. Both Richard II and one of Clarence's murderers in *Richard III* recall Pilate washing his hands; in the same play, one of the citizens quotes from Ecclesiastes. Even Iago refers to "holy writ" while Othello speaks of the curse upon the serpent and St. Peter's custody of the gates of heaven. King Claudius feels the curse of Cain upon him, and at the end of *Richard II* Bolingbroke sends Exton, who has killed the king for him, to wander with Cain through the shades of night. The Book of Numbers is cited by name in *Henry V* (I, 2), and 2 Peter is quoted from in French (III, 7). *All's Well That Ends Well* is rich in religious references. It is possible, though by no means certain, that the title of *Measure for Measure* may have been derived from Matthew 7:1.[2] But of course the character who is given the largest number of Biblical and religious citations is that notable Christian Sir John Falstaff,[3] who is "as poor as Job . . . but not so patient." He speaks of Adam, of Pharaoh's lean kine, and of both Dives and Lazarus in the parable and calls a tailor "a whoreson Achitophel."

Nuns and friars are important in *Romeo and Juliet* and *Measure for Measure*, but there is an Abbess even in the pagan *Comedy of Errors*. Generally speaking, the clergy are treated neither more nor less sympathetically than the laity; though I find no suggestion of what was later to be called anticlericalism, Shakespeare certainly did not regard clergymen with star-dust in his eyes. Sir Nathaniel

[2] See R. W. Chambers' Christian interpretation of this play in his British Academy Lecture of 1937, "The Jacobean Shakespeare and *Measure for Measure*," reprinted in his book, *Man's Unconquerable Mind* (Jonathan Cape, 1939).

[3] In the *Henry IV* plays; there are only a few such references in *The Merry Wives of Windsor*.

123

(*Love's Labour's Lost*) and Sir Hugh (*The Merry Wives of Windsor*) are hardly very respectworthy ambassadors for Christ. Portia knows it is a good divine that follows his own instructions, and even the unsophisticated Ophelia begs her brother not to counsel her like "ungracious pastors," that is, those lacking in Divine Grace. The Clown in *Twelfth Night*, donning the curate's robes to gull Malvolio, wishes he were the first to dissemble in such a gown.

Henry VIII has the monstrously worldly Cardinal Wolsey, and the historical plays in general are well supplied with politically minded warring prelates.[4] In *Richard III* the cowardly Cardinal Bourchier allows Buckingham, as Richard's minion, to violate sanctuary, thus helping Richard to dispose of the young princes. But the worst churchman in Shakespeare is undoubtedly Cardinal Pandulph, the completely cynical and unscrupulous ecclesiastical politician of *King John*, who is willing to sanction even murder when it serves his ends.

Of the references to specific Christian doctrines and beliefs, one of the most interesting is Isabella's reference to the Atonement:

> Why, all the souls that were were forfeit once;
> And He that might the vantage best have took
> Found out the remedy.[5]

Though God speaks in *The Winter's Tale* by the voice of Apollo's oracle at "Delphos," Polixenes still believes in the guilt "hereditary ours," and Cordelia's Gentleman refers to the "general curse/ Which twain have brought" into the world. Baptismal regeneration is mentioned in *Henry V*, and Helena of *All's Well* affirms her faith in God's omniscience. Imogen speaks of both grace and

---

[4] In Laurence Olivier's film production of *Henry V* the churchmen who justify the king's projected invasion of France were amusingly presented as half-senile hypocritical old duffers. Since this film was produced as an expression of English patriotism during World War II, this was somewhat surprising, but though it was undoubtedly effective for a modern audience, it can hardly be judged to have been Shakespeare's intention.

[5] See Frye's discussion of "Atonement," *op cit.*, 120–22, especially the passages cited from 2 *Henry VI* and *Richard III*. The sections on "Providence" (pp. 230–33) and "Repentance" (pp. 236–46) are also of very great interest.

despair and swears a Christian oath in " 'Ods pittikins"—God's little pity—but her prayer in Act III, Scene 2 is pagan, like Timon's prayer in Act IV, Scene 1 and, of course, Lear's curse upon Goneril. Perhaps there are more references to the life to come than to any other single idea. Fighting his way back from insanity, Lear mistakes Cordelia for a soul in bliss; Constance expects to see her child in heaven; in the Henry VI plays Margaret looks forward to greeting her partisans there, which certainly marks her one of the greatest religious optimists on record. Jessica thinks Bassanio so fortunate in his marriage to Portia that he must find "the joys of heaven here on earth." Desdemona and others are mindful of the importance of making their peace with God before death, though Emilia would "venture purgatory" for the fruits of adultery if the stakes were high enough. Mrs. Ford, on the other hand, is sure unchastity would send her to hell, and even Falstaff declares himself unwilling to endanger his soul for nothing. Olivia, too, has no difficulty conceiving the possibility of being damned for the love of Viola disguised as Cesario. There are also several references to the devil, some of them probably not intended to be taken literally.

In King John English nationalism stands opposed to the international Catholic Church with its powers of absolution and excommunication. It is true that this play is considerably less anti-Catholic than its source and that the King does finally submit to the church. Yet the rifling of the abbeys remains and the poisoning of the King by a monk, as well as the sinister character of Cardinal Pandulph, of which I have already spoken. All in all, scholars who believe Shakespeare to have been, or to have become, a Catholic[6] will not find much support in this play; his own irenic

---

[6] The case for Shakespeare as a Catholic is argued most elaborately in Heinrich Mutschmann and Karl Wentersdorf, Shakespeare and Catholicism (Sheed and Ward, 1952). Though I do not find the argument completely convincing, the book contains an exhaustive examination of Catholic references in the plays (or what the authors believe to be such) and much useful background information. Shakespeare's mother's family seems to have had Catholic connections. The tradition that "he died a papist" goes back to a Church of England clergyman, Richard Davies, c. 1700, and was accepted by the generally cautious Sir Edmund K. Chambers. But see Frye, 262, 275ff. for Shakespeare's mistakes in Catholic matters.

temperament is much more likely to have been responsible for the changes he made. Yet Tucker Brooke was certainly correct when he found the "religious penumbra" of the dramatist's mind "archaic." "For poetic purposes at least religion still connoted for him friars, masses, vigils, extreme unction, and purgatory. It came natural to him to invoke angels and ministers of grace, to swear by Our Lady and Saint Patrick." In some cases this may have been because he realized that the scene of his play had been laid in a Catholic country, though such considerations never weighed very heavily with him. As a dramatist, he may well have been more influenced by the superiority of Catholicism on the score of drama and picturesqueness.

Reformation controversies are sometimes glanced at. The Princess in *Love's Labour's Lost* (IV, 1) speaks of salvation by merit as "heresy," and Benedick refers to heretic martyrs. Sir Andrew Aguecheek hates Brownists, that is, religious independents, followers of Robert Brown, who believed in what is now called the Congregational polity in church government. Othello's Cassio is apparently a Calvinist, at least when he is drunk. "There be souls must be saved," he says, "and there be souls must not be saved." I do not know how much significance to attribute to Hamlet's attending the university at Martin Luther's Wittenberg, nor the apparent reference to the Diet of Worms in *Hamlet* (IV, 2), for the established religious background of this play is unmistakably Catholic.[7]

The real or fancied references to Puritanism are perhaps more interesting. Playwrights had a built-in interest in the Puritans, for they did not attend the theater and were doing their best to put it out of business. On the other hand, Shakespeare lodged in London with a Huguenot family, the Mountjoys, and the Huguenots were the French Puritans. After the dramatist's final return to Stratford, Puritanism was in the ascendant there, and he seems to have entertained a Puritan preacher on at least one occasion. It seems

---

[7] Frye believes that "Hamlet's references to theological doctrines . . . display a theological acumen quite appropriate to one whose education Shakespeare had ascribed to that original seat of Protestant learning, Wittenberg." *Op. cit.*, 161; see also p. 234.

clear that Shakespeare's daughter Susanna and her husband Dr. John Hall became Puritans,[8] and very likely Susanna's mother did also, or she may always have been one, since there are suggestions that the Hathaways were a Puritan family. The Geneva gown which the Puritans favored is certainly referred to in *All's Well*, and there have been those who thought they discerned attacks upon the Puritans in both *Twelfth Night* and *Measure for Measure*. Maria calls Malvolio "a kind of puritan." He has the Puritan attitude toward roistering and bear-baiting; he thinks nobly of the soul and consequently repudiates Pythagorean transmigration; Toby's references to him as possessed by the devil and urging him to pray are much funnier if we are to think of him as a Puritan. On the other hand, he has too much ambition and worldly vanity to be a good Puritan, and the portrait is hardly broad or obvious enough to be an effective satire or burlesque. We know of no instance in which Shakespeare has deliberately satirized any religious faith—whatever he himself believed, reverence was always, for him, the "angel of the world"—and Maria herself weakens the case for satire on the Puritans in Malvolio when she adds that "the devil a puritan that he is, or anything constantly but a time-pleaser."[9]

Angelo in *Measure for Measure* is another story. You can make a plausible case here if you are sufficiently ingenious, but the considerations involved are much more subtle, with consequently greater danger of error. Angelo tries to put immorality down by legal means and himself falls victim to his own passions. Only, of course, this has happened to a great many people besides Puritans. What the Freudians would presumably call Angelo's "suppressed desires" revenge themselves upon him through his onslaught upon Isabella, so that he commits a worse sin than any he has con-

---

[8] The inscription above Susanna's grave includes the following:

> Witty above her sex, but that's not all,
> Wise to salvation was good Mistress Hall,
> Something of Shakespeare was in that, but this
> Wholly of him with whom she's now in bliss.

[9] See A. H. Tolman, "Is Malvolio a Puritan?" in *Falstaff and Other Shakespearean Topics*.

demned. Shakespeare may have been riding the wave of the future here, but his interest seems centered upon the permanent problems and temptations of human nature rather than upon the vagaries of any sect or party.

The clearest references to Puritanism in Shakespeare are, not surprisingly, found in Falstaff. I have already spoken of his "damnable iteration," that is, his fondness for Scriptural references and quotations offered in a mocking or irreverent spirit. The Puritans used the word "vocation" to indicate a man's religious calling; Falstaff has a vocation too—stealing. Thus he prays God to give Poins the "spirit of persuasion" in order to induce Prince Hal to join in the robbery at Gadshill and to endow the Prince himself with "the ears of profiting."

Some of Shakespeare's plays are richer in religious references than others; among these are *Romeo and Juliet, Hamlet,* and *Macbeth.* In *Romeo and Juliet* we have the Friar, prayer, confession, shrines and pilgrims, "holy marriage," "God's bread" in the Mass, etc. Tybalt and Mercutio are killed on Easter Monday.

The Ghost of Hamlet's father comes from Purgatory,[10] where he is

> confin'd to fast in fires,
> Till the foul crimes done in my days of nature
> Are burnt and purg'd away.

Under any circumstances, his murder must have been "foul," but this murder was "most foul, strange, and unnatural" because he was

> Cut off even in the blossom of my sin,
> Unhousel'd, disappointed, unanel'd,[11]
> No reckoning made, but sent to my account
> With all my imperfections on my head.

---

[10] Though even this has, of late, provoked disagreement and controversy. Robert H. West canvasses the situation in "King Hamlet's Ambiguous Ghost," in his *Shakespeare and the Outer Mystery.*

[11] Without having received the sacrament, without having been given absolution, without having had the benefit of extreme unction. This is perhaps the most Catholic line in Shakespeare, and it is one of the curiosities of editorship that Pope, himself a Catholic, should have defined unaneled as meaning with no knell rung.

It is entirely logical therefore that Hamlet should pass up his opportunity to kill the King when he comes upon him at prayer because he wishes to take him in some act that has no relish of salvation in it, as ultimately he does. When the King rises from his knees, after Hamlet has passed on, the audience learns that he has not been successful in inducing a mood of true repentance, but Hamlet does not know this, and his ignorance deepens the irony of the situation. Hamlet also speaks of the Day of Doom and swears an oath by Saint Patrick. In the bitterness of his disillusionment not only about women but about life itself, he urges Ophelia to enter a nunnery. The conditions required for Christian burial are also canvassed in this play.

If in the Christian sense the only true tragedy is to forfeit one's soul, then *Macbeth* has a strong claim to be regarded as Shakespeare's most Christian tragedy. Certainly Christian references abound in it. Macbeth sees the winds as "fighting against the churches" and asks one of Banquo's murderers whether he is sufficiently "gospelled" to forgive Banquo for the wrongs that have been heaped upon him. Macbeth himself would "jump the life to come" and laments having given his "eternal jewel" to "the common enemy of man." The body of the murdered King is "the Lord's anointed temple." Banquo rests his case "in the great hand of God," and Lady Macbeth's doctor thinks she needs a "divine" more than a physician. Even the drunken Porter, opening the doors of Macbeth's castle, plays that he is admitting souls into hell, which, in view of what has just happened there, comes closer to the truth than he realizes.

II

Shakespeare's basic Christianism expresses itself also in his references to spiritual matters not directly connected with Christian doctrine. "The supernatural (or, as he would say, the 'metaphysical')," says Fripp, "the symbolic and suggestive, are everywhere." Stoll long ago convincingly argued that all the ghosts in Shakespeare are "real" (as are also, in a different sense, the

soothsayers, having no imposter among them).[12] So far as the ghosts are concerned, it is difficult to see how this could ever have needed to be argued, for the ghost appeared on the stage, in material reality, in broad daylight, in the person of a flesh-and-blood actor; surely it must have required far more subtlety and imagination than Shakespeare could safely count on in his audiences to see him as delusion. Those modern productions in which the supernatural manifestations are shadows, or interpreted as projections of some figment of the characters' minds are therefore quite un-Shakespearean in this aspect. The failure of such as Lady Macbeth and Hamlet's mother to see the ghosts which manifest in their presence is no factor, for according to Elizabethan and, so far as I know, all occult belief, a ghost can manifest to one who is *en rapport* with him and be quite invisible to everybody else. *Macbeth* and *Hamlet* are the tragedies most steeped in supernaturalism (as *Othello* is by all means the most naturalistic). A *Midsummer Night's Dream* has ghosts "wandering here and there" who "troop home to churchyards" at cockcrow in accord with the traditional belief, but *faerie* is the dominant note in the *Dream* while magic dominates *The Tempest*. The most extensive ghost scene in Shakespeare is in *Richard III* (V, 3), where Richard's victims appear to curse him and bless Richmond before the battle of Bosworth Field; Caesar's ghost serves a similar function by appearing to Brutus before Philippi. *Richard III* also contains the most elaborately narrated dream in Shakespeare—that of Clarence in Act I, Scene 4, though no doubt Romeo's dream moves us more. "Portents" on earth and in the skies precede Caesar's murder, but it is recognized that these must be "construed," and there are other portents the night King Duncan is killed and in *Richard III* and the *Henry VI* plays.

The reality of ghostly *manifestations* was taken for granted in Shakespeare's time, yet there was no universally accepted explanation of the phenomena which appeared. Catholics took one view, Protestants another, and there were of course hyperskeptics who

12 E. E. Stoll, "The Ghosts," in *Shakespeare Studies.*

gravitated toward what would now be called rationalism.[13] The idea that ghosts were masquerading demons, clothing themselves in the bodies of the departed, was common; it could never have occurred to any Elizabethan that Hamlet's desire to test the Ghost before acting finally and irrevocably upon his commands needed in any way to be apologized for, or that it must be regarded as a subterfuge, a device to delay action on the part of "a man who could not make up his mind," as Sir Laurence Olivier declared in his *Hamlet* film.

Varieties of belief and unbelief appear in the plays also. In *The Merry Wives of Windsor* Ford's antagonism toward the "old woman of Brentford," whom he regards as a witch, is probably intended merely to show him as a hard-headed middle-class man, and Hotspur passionately rejects all superstition primarily because of his antagonism toward the over-credulous Glendower. Horatio's initial skepticism about the ghost of Hamlet's father, and his immediate conversion as soon as he has laid eyes upon it, serves to disarm any possible incredulity in the audience. I do not, however, see that any dramatic purpose is served by having Antigonus of *The Winter's Tale* disavow the belief that "the spirits o' the dead/ May walk again" just before the bear gobbles him up. Nor do I know why Margery Jordan, the materializing medium of *2 Henry VI*, is called a witch, but the same mistake has been made for centuries with the "Witch of Endor" in the Bible. Richard III characteristically uses the belief of others in the supernatural to serve his own selfish ends, and the pretended healing of Simpcox

---

[13] For Elizabethan spiritualism, see Madeleine Doran, "That Undiscovered Country," *Philological Quarterly*, XX (1941), 413–27, the introduction and appendix to the J. Dover Wilson–May Yardley edition of Lewes Lavater's *Of Ghostes and Spirites Walking by Night* (OUP, 1929) and, in another connection, W. C. Curry, "The Demonic Metaphysics of *Macbeth*," *Studies in Philology*, XXX (1933), 395–426, reprinted in *Shakespeare's Philosophical Patterns*. Hamlet's reference, in the suicide soliloquy, to "the undiscover'd country from whose bourn/ No traveller returns" may seem a little surprising coming from a man whose actions are motivated by a commission received from a ghost. It is possible, however, that he may have meant "returns" in the sense of returning to life upon this earth, or possibly Shakespeare was for the moment thinking of the human problem in general rather than of Hamlet's specifically.

in 2 *Henry VI* leads to a good farce scene in the spirit of *Gammer Gurton's Needle*.

It may be of interest to glance briefly at Shakespeare's treatment of a special problem in Christian ethics—that of suicide. There is a fair number of suicides in his plays, and some of these, notably Romeo and Juliet, are treated very sympathetically, but the dramatist's general attitude is certainly disapproving. He recognized the difference between the Christian and the ancient Roman attitude toward suicide. In *The Rape of Lucrece* (ll. 1156ff.), he has the heroine discuss her projected self-murder at length, only to reach what I at least would describe as a thoroughly illogical and quixotic conclusion. Cleopatra finally decides that

> it is great
> To do the thing that ends all other deeds,

but even she is made first to consider whether it is not sinful

> To rush into the secret house of death
> Ere death dare come to us.

Cassius glorifies suicide in *Julius Caesar* (I, 3) as the final refuge against tyrants; so, later, does the Earl of Gloucester in *King Lear*, but he finally repents of his frustrated attempt to destroy himself. Portia, the noble wife of Brutus, is clearly not herself when she swallows fire; this is not the high Roman act but merely a pitiful mental breakdown.

In his very first soliloquy Hamlet laments that "the Everlasting" had "fix'd/ His canon 'gainst self-slaughter," which did not, however, prevent him from discussing suicide at length in the "To be or not to be" soliloquy, whose conclusion seems to be that the risk of future punishment is too great. Shakespeare would, therefore, seem to have been under the impression that there was some definite prohibition of suicide in the Bible, which is not the case, though this would, presumably, be embraced in the larger commandment "Thou shalt not kill." There is very little suicide in the Bible, and Jewish and Christian feeling has always run strongly against it. Barbarous, old-time burying customs survive in *Hamlet*,

though we had previously been under the impression that Ophelia's death was an accident, and there is a wryly humorous demand for social justice in the feeling of the gravediggers that she is getting more than she deserved because she was a gentlewoman, "and the more pity that great folk should have countenance in this world to drown or hang themselves, more than their even Christian." Equal rights for poor suicides is the gravedigger's plea, which, I suppose, is no more nor less reasonable than some of the others we have heard. The most senseless attempted suicide in Shakespeare is that of Horatio, "more an antique Roman than a Dane," when he belies everything we have been told about his stability by trying to follow Hamlet, and if there is any one which has a quality of atonement about it, it must be Othello's; we should think less of him, I believe, if he had been able to go on living after what he had done to Desdemona. It is different with Lady Macbeth, whose suicide, like Portia's, is the result of a breakdown, though here too, she would certainly have been a worse woman than she was if she had been able to take her sin in stride.

III

Though the problem cannot be discussed in detail here, it is difficult to consider Shakespeare's spiritual attitude without some reference to what have been called the "reconciliation plays" with which he closed his dramatic career.

In each of the three which are wholly the work of the dramatist[14] [writes Albert H. Tolman]—*Cymbeline, The Winter's Tale,* and *The Tempest*—there are wrong-doing and estrangement; but after sin and suffering comes peace, the peace of forgiveness. In *The Winter's Tale* we are back in the country again; we see the festival of the sheep-shearing and the wild flowers of the Avon meadows. "The wheel is come full circle." . . . The gracious, queenly women who here smile upon us are the choicest embodiments of human nobleness, of moral beauty, in all literature. In Miranda, Imogen, Perdita, and

[14] The one generally considered Shakespearean only in part is *Pericles.*

Hermione, we have a vision of "The crowning race of human-kind."

The traditional interpretation of this phenomenon, as expressed notably by such writers as Dowden and Furnivall and accepted in some form by most of the late nineteenth- and early twentieth-century critics was that the change represented Shakespeare's own spiritual development. Having passed through the *Sturm und Drang* reflected in his great tragedies, he had now shifted the currents of his life to deeper channels and accepted the universe. Dowden called the final period "On the Heights," in sharp contrast to the tragic period, "In the Depths." Even the generally cautious Chambers speculated dangerously at this point. Chambers attributed both the fierce pessimism of *Timon of Athens* and its incomplete state to the assumption that Shakespeare suffered a breakdown while working on it, after which he experienced a religious conversion. Dover Wilson would not have the conversion; he preferred to believe that the dramatist recovered his balance in some such manner as Wordsworth did when, after his disillusionment with the French Revolution, he fell in love with the Lake Country.

The rival interpretation was pioneered by Ashley H. Thorndike,[15] when he argued that instead of writing to express his own moods, Shakespeare was simply meeting current fashions in theatrical entertainment. When the tragedy of blood was popular, he wrote *Hamlet*; now that Beaumont and Fletcher had brought in a more romantic type of play, he felt it necessary to meet this competition. But Felix Schelling argued[16] that the priority of *Philaster* was speculative and that if there was any interdependence at this point, Beaumont and Fletcher may well have imitated Shakespeare, the established writer.

These views are not necessarily quite mutually exclusive. They are also subject to considerable variation. Lytton Strachey's essay

[15] *The Influence of Beaumont and Fletcher on Shakespeare* (Press of Oliver B. Wood, 1901).
[16] *Elizabethan Drama* (HM, 1908).

on "Shakespeare's Final Period"[17] is a convenient illustration of the confusion into which it is easy to fall. At the outset, Strachey seems to be arguing that the romances are no different from the plays Shakespeare had written earlier. He accuses critics of overstressing their idealistic aspects and overlooking the evil contained in them. But this is quite beside the point. Nobody has ever claimed that there is no evil in the romances; the point is simply that evil does not have the last word. (Without the presence of evil, there could have been no problem and therefore no need for reconciliation. Grace can only abound where sin has abounded first.) Later Strachey seems to assume that there was a change in Shakespeare's tone, but he finds it less attractive than his predecessors had found it. Even Shakespeare's style shows that he was now getting "bored with people, bored with real life, bored with drama, bored, in fact, with everything except poetry and poetical dreams." There can be no question about the intense condensation of the style or the free use of ellipsis and mixed constructions which occurs in it, and Chambers himself is in partial agreement with Strachey when he speaks of "these complicated and incoherent periods, . . . softened and unaccentuated rhythms, . . . tender and evanescent beauties" which were perhaps "the natural outcome of relaxed mental energies, shrinking from the effort after the wrought and nervous rhythms of the past." But is this boredom or a fresh burst of energy, rebelling against the fixed conventions and limitations of language? Shakespeare had never been the English equivalent of an academician, if there is such a thing.

Personally I should not be willing to admit without qualification that evil has the last word even in the tragedies. On the contrary, it is always, as Alden once remarked, "abnormal," with the universe itself "on the side of good."[18] Hamlet and Claudius die together, but nobody ever doubts that it is better to be Hamlet than Claudius. Cordelia, hanged in prison, glorifies human nature as her evil sisters defile it. Both Lear and Gloucester "achieve a

[17] Books and Characters (HB, 1922).
[18] Raymond Macdonald Alden, Shakespeare (Duffield, 1922), 349.

being, a ripeness, that might seem familiar to any reader of Aquinas or Hooker or the prayer book." Surely, as Robert H. West goes on, "if . . . Shakespeare intended no appeal to Christian ideas of a man born again and serene in God's peace, he went strangely out of his way." Shakespeare was not playing the Glad Game. It is corruption that his good people escape; they do not always escape death. Neither did Christ. "The world of Shakespeare's comedies of forgiveness," says Robert Grams Hunter, "is one where hate and love are opposed to each other in a precarious balance which only just permits the ascendancy of love and order."[19] Actually, none of the ideas with which we have concerned ourselves here are peculiar to the romances; the idea of forgiveness is almost as important in the Sonnets, which most people do not think of first of all for their religious significance.[20] There are even times when it is mercy to the undeserving that is peculiarly touching ("Why, all the souls that were were forfeit once"). Bradley, impressed by the heavy stress upon the frown of the great, the tyrant's stroke, slander, and censure rash in the famous song in *Cymbeline*, ventures that Shakespeare was so mindful of the perpetual need for forgiveness that "he had not at all strongly . . . that instinct and love of justice and retribution which in many are so powerful," and this may well be true. Perhaps he might even have agreed with William Dean Howells that no man is wise enough to be just. His only choice is between kindness and cruelty.

There *is* a difference in tone, then, between the romances and the earlier comedies and tragedies, but the difference is a development, not a revolution. Distinctions grow clearer and clearer until they culminate in *The Tempest*, where Prospero is almost a god-like figure. For him "the rarer action is/ In virtue than in vengeance," and once having won his enemies, he will not "burden his remembrance" or theirs with "a heaviness that's gone."[21] In

[19] *Shakespeare and the Comedy of Forgiveness* (Columbia University Press, 1965), 245.

[20] An important exception is George Herbert Palmer's charming Ingersoll Lecture, *Intimations of Immortality in the Sonnets of Shakspere* (HM, 1912).

[21] Prospero's "Our revels now are ended" speech has occasioned some difficulty. "The thought in the hero's mind," says Stoll, "is not only of death but of ultimate

Greene's *Pandosto,* which was the source of *The Winter's Tale,* the character who corresponds to Leontes kills himself after having narrowly escaped committing incest; Shakespeare saves him from such corruption and keeps him alive for a better fate. I am sure Shakespeare kept in touch with changing fashions in the London theater, but he was a man, not a writing machine, and I do not believe he was unaware of the implications of what he had written.

universal dissolution, and of death as a sleep, and of life as a dream. The thought is not pursued by the poet—it steals upon him and whispers in his ear" (*Shakespeare Studies,* 23). It does considerably more, however, to some of the commentators. I see no justification for Donald A. Stauffer's feeling that Shakespeare "lived so long in imaginary worlds which were necessarily his worlds as a creative artist, that distinctions were lost, that all experience became imaginary, and that not only the great globe but religion itself could be conceived only as a noble dream" (*Shakespeare's World of Images* [Norton, 1949], 364).

VII

SOME CONCLUSIONS

In contemporary records and in tradition, Shakespeare is gentle, civil, upright, sweet, honorable, agreeable, honest, generous of mind and mood, open and free, pleasant, witty, and of good company. It is obvious that "gentle" means something more here than its usual meaning today, embracing what we think of as all the qualities of a cultivated, generous gentleman. Though he could go to law if necessary when his rights were invaded, he was no quarreler, for he held himself aloof not only from riots and duels (which caused so much trouble for his friend Ben Jonson) but from literary squabbles as well. Chettle publicly apologized to him for his share in publishing Robert Greene's attack upon him early in his career, and Jaggard reported him "much offended" over the appearance of *The Passionate Pilgrim*. We do not know what if anything Shakespeare did in the War of the Theaters, but if he was in it at all, he was on the periphery, and tradition credits him with having ended it, not provoked it. Clearly he had friends who valued his company, but it is hard to be sure how much they saw of him; his refusal to be "debauched" and the convenient illnesses he suffered when invited out by roisterers must, one would think, have put a crimp on his social activities in London, and for all the

fame of "the wit-combats betwixt him and Ben Jonson, like a Spanish great galleon and an English man of war," we have no real evidence that these ever took place.[1] Fuller, who speaks of them, was not born until 1608 and thus could not possibly have witnessed them, and we have no picture of Shakespeare at the Mermaid or any other tavern from any contemporary witness.

Only a fool could argue that Shakespeare was in any sense a phlegmatic person. He certainly did not, as Henry James observed of George Eliot's Adam Bede, lack "spontaneity and sensibility" and "the capacity to be tempted." On the contrary, Masson found his interest in nature and human nature boundless; he "pierces into" things on all sides with "shivering intensity," understanding them and "translating them to the very heart." Sir Leslie Stephen felt[2] that in view of this abnormal sensitiveness, his achievement of "a prosperous and outwardly commonplace career" was all the more remarkable. He might have been a Pistol or a Falstaff; instead he became "a highly respectable man as well as a world-poet." The rich fertility of his imagination alone shows how great his endowment was: Mercutio's Queen Mab speech is only one of a hundred examples of his capacity to pour out a hundred instances or illustrations where one would do. But, unlike most sensitive people, he did not spend his time nursing his own sensitivities; instead he used them as a means to find his way into the hearts and minds of others.

Moreover, his imagination is, on the whole, warm, genial, and sunny. "I wake with a start," writes John Jay Chapman, "when the shade of Dante looks in at the cottage window where I had fallen asleep with a copy of *Twelfth Night* in my hand."[3] This is not the whole truth, but there is truth in it. Is it an accident that the accepted canon of Shakespeare's plays comprises ten tragedies, ten "histories," and *seventeen* comedies? It may be so, but I doubt it. King John's scornful reference to "that idiot, laughter," which will

---

[1] See Stoll, *Shakespeare Studies*, 7–8.
[2] *Studies of a Biographer*, Second Series, Vol. IV (Putnam, 1902).
[3] A *Glance toward Shakespeare* (The Atlantic Monthly Press, 1922).

> keep men's eyes
> And strain their cheeks to idle merriment—
> A passion hateful to my purposes,

is quite in character; without it he would not be the villain he is. How wonderful is Cleopatra's humor, even at the doors of death.

> Hast thou the pretty worm of Nilus there,
> That kills and pains not?

she asks the Clown. "Will it eat me?" Even with her last agony upon her, her humor does not desert her:

> O, couldst thou speak,
> That I might hear thee call great Caesar ass
> Unpolicied!

But perhaps an even more audacious example has occurred a little earlier when she and her women are drawing the dying Antony up into the monument:

> Here's sport indeed! How heavy weighs my lord!
> Our strength is all gone into heaviness,
> That makes the weight.

To be sure, there is gain as well as loss involved in committing one's self to a humorous attitude toward life. Comedy always presupposes a social standard, and if the humorous man is unlikely to fornicate in the marketplace at midday, he is equally unlikely to become the leader of an unpopular moral crusade. To achieve that one must be willing to be laughed at, becoming a fool for Christ's sake (Saint Paul said that the preaching of the Cross was foolishness to them that perish). Comedy, consequently, though certainly an enemy to vice, can hardly be called without qualification an ally of morality. Comedy opposes vice because it is excessive, immoderate, unbalanced. But it opposes excessive virtue on the same score: "Be not righteous overmuch; neither make thyself over wise: why shouldst thou destroy thyself? Be not over much wicked, neither be thou foolish; why shouldst thou die before thy

time?"[4] The discrepancy between the real and the ideal has always been a favorite theme in comedy, and if the comic dramatist has been less concerned with immoderate virtue than with vice, the reason doubtless is that there is no oversupply of the former commodity in the world.

It was not only for fear of being debauched, however, that Shakespeare held himself apart; he seems to have been one of those rare men who combine perfect friendliness with a capacity for keeping the citadel of the personality untouched. It is not easy to picture him upon a psychiatrist's couch, or even whispering secrets to a friend at the latter end of a seacoal fire. His will itself is probably the most impersonal such document ever drawn up; there is no hint of emotion or idiosyncrasy in it. Chettle did not know him personally at the time he apologized to him for Greene's attack, and Greene himself had regarded him as an outsider. When the Mountjoys got into trouble and Shakespeare was called upon to testify in court, he developed an excellent forgettery. Except as a business man and a Stratfordian, he never belonged to a group. And even in Stratford, we need only compare his involvement with his father's to be sure that he still maintained a certain distance even there.

In a sense, he seems even to have held himself apart from his work. It is impossible to believe that he could have produced it without realizing its value, but is it not almost as inconceivable that he could have done so without making any effort to preserve it? In *Hyperion* Longfellow has the Baron tell Paul Flemming that "what we call miracles and wonders of art are not so to him who created them, for they were created by the natural movement of his own great soul." I am not pretending that Shakespeare had Longfellow's temperament, though this was less mild than many persons imagine, but surely he did not take himself with undue seriousness or overestimate the value and importance of his work in comparison with the totality of life. Pope's emphasis was wrong when he wrote of Shakespeare that he

4 Ecclesiastes 7:16–17.

141

For gain not glory winged his roving flight,
And grew immortal in his own despite,

but it is impossible to believe that the writer who "never blotted out a line" adhered to the "Oh, the pain of it!" school of creators, and I for one do not believe that he was unable to eat his dinner even after having written the last act of *King Lear*. Moreover, I believe that he was a greater, not a lesser, artist because of this superb control.

It is said that when a Caruso record was played for a physicist, he exclaimed, "Dead center!" and that a metaphysician murmured, "If God had a voice . . . ." Shakespeare's resolute retention of his own individuality makes his marvelous centrality all the more wonderful and encourages us to hope that he prefigures the man of the future, though we may be sure that it will be a long time yet before we overtake him. Coleridge expressed it by saying that he keeps "at all times in the high road of life," with no "innocent adulteries," "virtuous vice," "benevolent butchers," or "sentimental rat-catchers." He assumed free will out of his necessities as a dramatist and held his characters responsible for their actions, since that is the only basis upon which a character can be made to interest an audience, and he held the mirror up to nature not because he anticipated the naturalists in their "slice of life" theories but as a means of raising a standard by which men might measure themselves and to which they might adhere.[5] But if sane dramatists are obliged to make these assumptions, are not also sane men?

There is loss here as well as gain, for Shakespeare was a man, not a god. If everybody is wiser than anybody, somebody may still perceive truths which everybody misses. We cannot enjoy the benefits of revolution and the comforts of the established order simultaneously. But though revolutionists are sometimes necessary, they are not comfortable, and they often destroy more than they create.

Shakespeare's shortcomings in revolutionary perceptions were

[5] See Frye, 267–68.

then inextricably bound up with his genius; we could not amend him in this matter without throwing him into the caldron to be melted and molded anew. Nor are these considerations without their bearing upon the considerably mooted matter of his religion. Some have been disturbed by the fact that he makes so little profession of faith. But he is no more reserved about religious matters than he is about everything else which concerned himself intimately. If he must be set down as not believing in God because he does not talk about Him, he might, on the same basis, be accused of not believing in William Shakespeare.

Those who believe he was a Catholic might reasonably supply him with motives for religious reserve upon this score. Personally I should not be distressed to conceive him thus. Catholicism would well suit his centrality, for what is more central in Western civilization than the Catholic faith? I could even feel that simply because he might reasonably regard basic matters as settled to a greater extent than a Protestant could, a Renaissance Catholic who was neither a devotee nor a specialist in theology might, for that very reason, feel more free to give his attention to secular matters and the affairs of this world. My only difficulty is the absence of satisfactory evidence to prove Shakespeare a Catholic, combined with the presence of a good deal which seems to indicate that he was a satisfied member of the Church of England. For that matter, I have always felt, too, that the, in some ways, Shakespearean Sir Walter Scott "ought" to have been a Catholic, yet we know that he was not, nor indeed very sympathetic toward the Catholic Church.

Obviously some of this must be conjectural, and a hyperskeptical reader may perhaps urge that we know so little about how Shakespeare spent his time that it is still possible that he went to bed drunk every night with a different woman. One need not, however, commit oneself to the unlikeliest possible hypothesis. We do not know all about the iceberg from having seen only that part of it which rises above the water, but we may be very sure that what we do not see is neither a cathedral nor a nudist colony. We know how hard Shakespeare worked and what he produced. We

are familiar with the position he won for himself in society and how his fellows regarded him. Above all, we have the plays themselves, and their beauty, their normality, their nobility, and their basic Christianism have always been recognized by every reader who was not hopelessly off center himself. Moreover, there is nothing in what we do know about Shakespeare's life which undercuts the impressions we receive from the plays. Gossip there has been aplenty, but it is all of the "it seems" or "somebody has said" variety, and trying to pin it down is, to use Theodore Roosevelt's figure, like trying to nail currant jelly to the wall. Caroline Spurgeon seems sentimental when she calls Shakespeare "Christlike" in character, and she gets on very thin ice indeed when she proceeds to declare that "he does not seem to have drawn any support from the forms and promises of conventional religion, nor does he show any sign of hope or belief in a future life." It remains true nevertheless that if there were dark places in Shakespeare's life, those to whom it seems very important to make us aware of them have hitherto been very unfortunate in both their arguments and the materials they have had to work with. There is nobody in secular history at least to whom we owe more than we do to Shakespeare; neither is there anybody of whom we know less evil.

APPENDIX A:

GAMALIEL BRADFORD'S
PSYCHOGRAPH OF SHAKESPEARE*

The interesting thing about Shakespeare is that the greatest poet of the world was not a learned scholar, not a highly trained professional artist or thinker, but just a common, everyday man, beginning life on a simple, everyday plane. He made his way, his success, his fortune, without pretense to great genius or to being in any way different from the people around him. The secret of his power of creation was his infinite and inexhaustible love of life, of all life. He tolerated the evil with the good, with an infinite curiosity, because he himself was human and he felt that everything human, strength and weakness, vice and virtue, was akin to him. He was enthralled, intoxicated by the beauty, the glory, the richness of this actual world.

Shakespeare was born on the twenty-third of April, 1564, in the little town of Stratford-on-Avon. His father was a well-to-do tradesman, of a respected family, but he had a number of children and his business affairs did not always go well. William had the education of an average boy of his class at that period. He was more or less drilled in Latin, and

* From *Portraits and Personalities*, by Gamaliel Bradford, edited by Mabel A. Bessey (Houghton Mifflin Company, 1933). Reprinted by permission of the publishers.

145

had, probably, some knowledge of French and a little of Italian, but there was never any question of a university training for him.

It has always been a stumbling-block for critics that what appears to be the vast learning involved in Shakespeare's plays should have been accumulated by one who had had so little formal intellectual discipline. It is necessary, therefore, to distinguish here. It is true that the varied drama of Shakespeare touches almost all subjects under heaven and, in touching these subjects, displays a surprising amount of information about them. But the information is not that of the trained, systematic scholar. It is often inaccurate and always irregular. In other words, it is precisely what would be gathered by a man of natural quickness, or extraordinary aptness of wit, who went about in the world everywhere, and kept his eyes and his ears open at all times. The difference, too, between those days and ours must be remembered. There were no newspapers. People did not get their information much from print. What knowledge they did have, they got from talk, from observation, in short, just from living. It was said of that other great spirit, Abraham Lincoln, that he "learned by sight, scent, and hearing." It was in just that way that Shakespeare learned, and his education was the education of life.

It was the education of a furiously active life from the start. He liked play, pranks and frolics, movement and pleasure, and if he did not like work any more than most boys, he had the large, farseeing wisdom to appreciate that work was useful, even for those who relished play.

He did not stay long in Stratford. Life was not rich enough for him there, not sufficiently splendid with opportunity. Possibly he explained to Anne Hathaway, the woman he had married when he was eighteen, that a few months in London would send him back to her with a fortune. Perhaps she believed him—perhaps not. At any rate in 1586, Shakespeare went to London and although the fortune did not come quite so rapidly as he wished, opportunities were obviously dazzling, and life was so varied and so gorgeous that for the time personal fortune was lost sight of.

It was just the time of the defeat of the Spanish Armada, the very height of the great days of Queen Elizabeth. All the splendor of the Renaissance imagination had drifted across the Channel and London was seething and boiling with great poets—and great ambitions. Into this world of color and splendor and furious activity, Shakespeare plunged with all the ardor of twenty and all the curiosity of his intense

and vigorous spirit. It was natural that he should drift to the theater, for in those days when printing was slow and difficult and the public was so concentrated as to be accessible by word of mouth, the theater was the most effective mode of expression. But from all tradition tells us, it would appear that his approach to that mysterious and complicated theatrical world was as difficult as it would be for any country boy today, if he had nothing but his native gifts and energy to back him. The story runs of his carrying torches as link-boy to light the great and rich as they made their way about the streets at night. From that he gradually worked his way into the theater by the back door, later became an actor in small parts, and in this manner familiarized himself with every detail of stage management which is essential to anyone who would make a business of theatrical writing. There is various reference to Shakespeare's own acting, as if he kept it up with assiduity, but there is no indication of any marked success in this line, such, for instance, as attended the careers of his friends Alleyn and Burbage.

On the other hand, it soon became evident that the pen rather than the actual stage was his means of success. Here the man's quick practical tact and infinite adaptability were at once manifest. He did not attempt at first, as so many playwrights do, to carry out his own ideas, obstinately, without regard to the wishes or the work of others. There were a lot of old, worn-out plays lying about the theaters. Why should not somebody make them over, revamp them? Certainly, said Shakespeare. And he was just the man to do it, and he would do it, for he perceived at once that nothing could be more helpful to him in learning his trade. He took the old historical plays, of Kyd, perhaps, or Greene, or Peele, or even Marlowe, made them over, tinkered them, added a few scenes, or speeches, or even startling lines, of his own, and made them live. His success did not always increase his popularity with friends of the authors, whose plays he revivified; still, in that age of furious literary quarrels, he managed to keep on fairly friendly terms with most people, for there was in him something eminently and irresistibly lovable. Consequently, in the company which afterward so long held and operated the Globe Theater he soon established a secure position and, as time went on, one which proved very lucrative.

It soon became obvious that such an energetic, creative, imaginative temperament would not long be satisfied with making over the productions of others, but would be restlessly impelled to put its own experiences and hopes and passions into creations of its own. Of these,

147

the first attempts were necessarily timid and tentative and imitative. There was Plautus, whom Shakespeare had read at school. Surely one might make a modern play out of Plautus. And Plautus, with a fullness of modern touches, furnished the quips and quibbles of the *Comedy of Errors*. And there were Italian tales, which the busy youth read at odd hours. Perhaps romances might be spun out of those, romances like *The Two Gentlemen of Verona*, with its gentle, bewildered, bewildering lovers, inextricably entangled in the strange, bewildering tangle of life. But, after all, even better than these vagaries of his reading, he found it might be possible to draw on the depths of his own experience, to make strange, exciting, diverting, picturesque dramas out of just the things that he had seen and known. Immediately the young playwright turned back to the things of his boyhood, his school-days, the queer pedants who taught him, and all the queer, fantastic legends they had liked to teach and trifle with. So he made plays like *Love's Labour's Lost*, with the garrulous teacher, Holofernes, and the tricksy schoolboy, Moth, and an academic flavor of charming, super-fluous learning pervading the whole. Again, he turned to the world of dreams, and interwove the dreams with all the lovely out-of-door life that had penetrated his soul in the wandering Stratford days. Out of this, with just a touch of tragic and comic classic legend, he framed the delicate, airy fabric of *A Midsummer Night's Dream*, with its dancing, lilting, shadowy fairies, and its intricate web of evanescent grace.

Again, he argued, if he was going to put his own laughter and his own dreams on the stage, why not put his own passion there too, his own desperate wrestle with youth and life. For already he was beginning to understand that his struggle was simply the struggle of anyone in the world and if he depicted his, honestly, sincerely, the world could not help listening to him as if it were listening to its own. To be sure, there is no reason to consider *Romeo and Juliet* directly autobiographical, nor need we look for any trace of Anne Hathaway in the girlish, passion-ate daughter of the Capulets. There was still the clinging habit for Italian story, someone else's story, which was to stay with Shakespeare to the end. But despite this fact, through it all, there is the throb and thrill of intense personal experience. That boy who is looking for love, with no definite idea of what he wants; that girl, whose idea is even less definite than the boy's, yet who, the instant she is confronted with her destiny, cries out,

Go, ask his name.—If he be married,
My grave is like to be my wedding-bed—

that wild tempest of fate which whirls them together for a few mad,
dreamy instants, and then whirls them apart again; that storm of passion unfulfilled which transforms the boy and girl into man and
woman and then sweeps them out of life, shaking

... the yoke of inauspicious stars
From this world-wearied flesh

proclaims in every line of the play reality in the life of Shakespeare
before it was transformed into immortal verse.

For it is the peculiar greatness of the drama of Shakespeare and of his
age that life is really lived before it is made into drama at all. In other
great dramas, life is introduced for action and for dramatic purposes.
In Shakespeare, life crowds in, pushes in, bursts in, right in the middle
of the dramatic action, just for itself and for the splendor of its vital
reality. In all these early plays, as it is in the later ones, Shakespeare was
profoundly, passionately interested in the men and women he saw
about him. He loved their laughter, their tears, their prayers, their
oaths, all their passions and their hopes, and whether he intended
it or not, these things found their way into his pages. Thus his plays are
strewn everywhere with delicious minor characters, often having little
bearing on the action proper, but making it more real by their own
desperate reality and intensity. The chatter of Launce and Speed in
The Two Gentlemen of Verona may not be brilliant in itself, but it is
eloquent when one realizes that Shakespeare probably gathered it from
common lips at Stratford. The fooling of Bottom and his clowns in
A Midsummer Night's Dream is admirable as contrasted with the
dainty grace of the Fairy Queen; it is even more admirable as a close
portrayal of the village life that Shakespeare had known so well. Or
again, take Mercutio in *Romeo and Juliet*. Merely as a dramatic utility,
his part in the action is unimportant, but his wit, his gayety, his sparkle,
form a vivid impersonation of the young noblemen whom Shakespeare
had so often lighted home on winter nights.

It was all life, it was all Shakespeare's life, and we do not understand
him until we appreciate how intimately his life was interwoven with
his work and his work with his life, so closely indeed, that it is neces-

149

sary at all times to complement one with the other. What gives the unfailing vitality to the work is the sense that the man was living passionately and earnestly all the time. As a matter of actual fact, we know little enough about him, just occasional glimpses, coming from moldy documents, records of lawsuits or business contracts, but what we do know is sufficient to show that he was living, in every sense of the word, all the time as well as working. He steadily succeeded in worldly things, accumulating property as he went. He always seemed to keep an eye on the home center of Stratford, as if his real interests and loves were there, though he himself was so far away. He cared for his family, at a distance. He helped his father out of financial difficulties. London and the London theaters were his workshop; Stratford was his home, the place where he had been born and where he meant to die—when he got round to it.

But in the late fifteen-nineties, dying was a long way off and he had much to do first. There was life of all sorts to put on the stage, and for a time he was mainly busy with the gayer, sweeter sides of it. There was still the busy weaving of intricate, romantic plots, built perhaps on those same Italian and French stories, which always fascinated him, twisted tangles of lovers who stumbled through fretful difficulties before they fell into one another's arms, as in *Much Ado About Nothing* or the *Merchant of Venice*. In addition, there were wilder, richer medleys of dream fancy, like the twin complications of *Twelfth Night*, with its luster of golden revelry, and above all, of *As You Like It*, with its exquisite forest setting, where the wandering lovers

> Under the shade of melancholy boughs
> Lose and neglect the creeping hours of time.

Through all this, everywhere, there was the ever-growing consciousness of life, all the more fascinating, and bewildering, and insistent, because of its precariousness. There was always this bustling, huddling crowd and company of living figures, thronging, dancing, laughing, upon the varied stage, making drama and action even out of a hurly-burly by the very intensity and reality of their existence. There were the heroes and heroines, oddly contrasted: the men, whom Shakespeare had so closely and intimately touched and known, almost brutally real, of the earth, earthy, most of them hardly heroes at all; the women, the Portias, the Rosalinds, the Violas, ideal, exquisite, and well-nigh per-

fect, yet, curiously enough, giving the impression of reality as much as the men, all flesh and blood and all different.

Again, as in the earlier plays, and even more noticeable, there was the troop of minor characters, giving always that petulant, assertive sense of their own sweet, aggressive existence, not because the action or even the author required them, but because they chose to be there, and came and went, not at the author's will, but at their own. Typical, for example, is the Jaques of *As You Like It*, of even less importance in the story than Mercutio in *Romeo and Juliet*, yet weaving his melancholy reflections and cynical comments with irresistible grace into the gold and scarlet tissue of the lovers' adventures. And the stamp of the Shakespearean imagination sets its immortal touch upon even such momentary insignificance as the frail courtier, Le Beau, when he is made to murmur to Orlando,

> Hereafter, in a better world than this,
> I shall desire more love and knowledge of you.

There is the inexhaustible comic richness and fancy of such fooling as that of Sir Toby and Sir Andrew in *Twelfth Night* and the deeper richness of Falstaff in the Henry plays or in *Merry Wives of Windsor*.

Shakespeare's profound life instinct and life grasp shows itself perhaps most clearly in the skill with which he takes certain old, conventional, dramatic types, notably Falstaff, from the primitive braggart soldier of Latin comedy, and makes them living, breathing human beings who break away from convention of any type. The climax of this creative process culminates in the creation of the Shakespearean fool—Touchstone of *As You Like It*, or Feste of *Twelfth Night*. Others used the conception before Shakespeare, and others have used it since his time. No other has succeeded in breathing into it the marvelous combination of shrewd and penetrating insight with infinitely careless folly, of the eternal significance of the golden present moment and the futile, intangible evanescence of even that eternal moment itself.

Over all this web of comic grace and splendor is showered the glory of lyrical magic at which Shakespeare had tried his 'prentice hand in the poems of his youth. This transfigures even the most prosaic portions of the plays, and surely reaches its bewitching climax in the songs of *As You Like It* and *Twelfth Night*:

> What is love? 'Tis not hereafter.
> Present mirth hath present laughter;

What's to come is still unsure.
In delay there lies no plenty;
Then come kiss me, sweet and twenty,
Youth's a stuff will not endure.

All the time that this mighty process of creation was going on, we have the feeling that Shakespeare was growing and developing. Since we have nothing in the way of personal documents to go upon, we must, of course, cull this development from Shakespeare's work. Such interpretation of a man's work, moreover, has to be made with extreme caution, for we are obliged to distinguish the outward development of the work itself, influenced purely by circumstance, from the inward progress of the spirit. Nevertheless, it is impossible not to recognize something of this spiritual progress in the gradual modification of the dramatic product. Such a progress is obvious even in the more mechanical matters of meter and style. The rhythm of Shakespeare's earlier plays, taken over from Marlowe, is slow, stately, measured. But as life and the complicated subtlety of living got hold of him more and more, he released his form of expression, made his verse more flexible, more responsive, in a sense nearer to prose, yet always keeping the high-wrought stimulus of poetic movement at his command. So again, with the use of language. In petulant youth the unchecked imagination wrought freely and wildly, in extravagant conceits, soaring figures, which often went madly astray. As years brought more sober reflection, the conceits gave place to more intense, concentrated inward comment, and the style became close-knit, substantial, at moments almost weighted and freighted with the grave, so that in the later plays one is sometimes reminded of Shakespeare's own words,

And nature, as it grows again toward earth,
Is fashion'd for the journey, dull and heavy.

But this external and formal process of development is less important than the internal and spiritual one. Only in considering the latter, we have to be on our guard against mistaking mere conventions of the period for more personal conditions. Thus there is the puzzling problem of Shakespeare's Sonnets. Wordsworth said that with the sonnet, as a key, Shakespeare unlocked his heart. And in touches like,

Two loves I have of comfort and despair,

or,

Tir'd with all these, for restful death I cry,

we have a hint of intimate personal revelation. Yet the sonnet was at that time popular all over Europe, and everybody was pouring out personal revelation in it, often in a thoroughly conventional and artificial manner. It is impossible to say just how much this manner influenced Shakespeare.

Something of the same caution must be used in viewing the even more interesting point of the profound spiritual change of attitude suggested by the transition from the comic period of about 1600 to the Roman and intensely tragic group of plays that were scattered over the next six or eight years. Public taste was probably demanding work of a more serious and gloomy order, and Shakespeare was peculiarly quick to grasp what his audience wanted. Yet it is difficult not to believe that some violent tumult and disturbance in his own soul did not accompany the ardent, acute wrestling with the most terrible tragic problems of life that appears in *Macbeth*, with its fierce strife of ambition, *Othello*, with its incarnation of tormenting jealousy, *Lear*, with its paternal willfulness and filial ingratitude, and finally *Hamlet*, with its profound questioning of all the inmost secrets and mysteries of life itself. Shakespeare may have given such work a popular appeal, but it stands to reason that the man himself was pouring forth in these plays the deepest obscure workings of his own tragic experience.

Again, as with all the other periods and all the other forms, there is everywhere the secure, steadying, vivifying contact with the reality of life. All these varied tragedies are founded on old hazy legends, which might easily have become merely typical and conventional melodrama. But in every case, and most notably of all in *Hamlet*, Shakespeare takes the typical, legendary figure, and breathes a soul into it, makes it real, palpitating, alive, with a momentary existence as intense, as all-pervading as yours or mine, an existence that *is* yours or mine, and therefore takes hold of us with an extraordinary tenacity, an extraordinary power. And while, necessarily, in these plays of concentrated dramatic action, the one dominating figure is more important than the comedies, there is everywhere the same splendid horde of minor personages, each

existing for himself, in glorious independence, even to the fool, who would seem to be pre-eminently a creature of comedy, yet who, in the delightful name of Yorick, makes his way into *Hamlet*, and again in the nameless Fool of *Lear* achieves the supreme intrusion of folly in the acid dissolution of life.

After this tragic stage, with the three last plays, *The Tempest*, *Cymbeline*, and *The Winter's Tale*, we see a new Shakespeare. Here again the possibility of external influence confronts us, for it may be that Shakespeare changed his style to meet the exigencies of younger rivalry. Yet here again, there is some modification in the Shakespearean spirit. The suggestion of sunshine, of harmony, of reconciliation and serenity, that pervades these plays, must indicate a certain restoring of tranquillity, after the tragic tumult. With these qualities, it is impossible on the other hand to deny an element of falling off. Exquisite and even more finished as the execution is, elaborate as is the handling of the dramatic action, the poetry does not reach the same magnificent pitch. Above all, the characters do not thrill and throb with quite the same intensity of life. The fooling of Stephano in *The Tempest* is not the fooling of Feste in *Twelfth Night*.

The matter of supreme interest here is that, having reached this point, Shakespeare should have stopped short. Other great artists, Goethe, Beethoven, Scott, Browning, Meredith, outlived themselves, went on to the end, producing work that is great indeed, yet lamentably inferior to the masterpieces of their prime. Shakespeare stopped. Somewhere from 1610 to 1612, when he was still under fifty and apparently at the height of his physical and mental power, he wrote his last play. He had done his work, he had provided for his old age, he was secure in what he had accomplished, he was quite content to leave the field to others. Perhaps no element of his greatness impresses one more than such supreme self-control.

He returned to Stratford, settled himself among his old neighbors, and lived until his fifty-second birthday, April 23, 1616. We have no reason to suppose that he felt that he had solved the vast problems of life. On the contrary, the bearing of one of the latest passages of reflection that he has left us, the speech of Prospero, in *The Tempest*, seems to leave all the mysteries exactly where they were:

> And, like the baseless fabric of this vision,
> The cloud-capp'd towers, the gorgeous palaces,

The solemn temples, the great globe itself,
Yes, all which it inherit, shall dissolve,
And, like this insubstantial pageant faded,
Leave not a rack behind. We are such stuff
As dreams are made on, and our little life
Is rounded with a sleep.

But later, as earlier, we get the impression that to Shakespeare life, with
its endless present richness and variety, its evanescent, everlasting splendor, which only demands that we should meet it in the same spirit, is
enough. And when we leave it, we should leave it in the spirit of
Shakespeare's own magnificent lines:

Men must endure
Their going hence, even as their coming hither;
Ripeness is all.

APPENDIX B:

SHAKESPEARE HIMSELF
by John M. Manly*

Not many years ago it was currently admitted that the earth had a north pole and a south pole, but it was held that the difficulties of reaching either were so great that the task would probably never be accomplished. Yet both the north pole and the south have been reached.

To-day it is admitted by scholars as well as by the general public that somebody wrote the poems and plays commonly known as Shakespeare's, but it is doubted by many scholars whether it will ever be possible from the information at our disposal to determine what kind of man he was, what were his tastes, his special accomplishments, his main interests, and the experiences of life by which these were developed and cultivated. The difficulties which seem to lie in the way of such an inquiry are neither few nor insignificant. In the first place, the records and traditions remaining of the man himself and the impressions he made on his contemporaries, though more numerous than for almost any other dramatist of his time, still are too vague, too lacking in detail to be satisfactory to an age like ours, which in the case of its

* Reprinted from A Memorial Volume to Shakespeare and Harvey, University of Texas Bulletin, No. 1701, January 1, 1917.

favorite writers is mainly concerned with items of petty personal gossip
—where they will spend the summer, whether they write best in the
early morning or toward midnight, whether for breakfast food they
prefer rolled oats or baled hay. In the second place, the other sources
of information—the poems and plays themselves—offer special difficulties of interpretation.

The plays are dramatic, the poems are narrative and impersonal, and
the sonnets are said to be conventional and equally incapable of personal application. In no passage can we be sure, it is said, that the ideas
or the attitude expressed are the ideas or attitude of the author. His
dramatis personae say and do what is not only appropriate to them but
is the natural and inevitable expression of their own characters and
social experience. Furthermore, it is argued, the various characters in
the plays display a range of experiences and of technical knowledge
covering every field of human activity and thought; and consequently
we cannot infer anything in regard to the author's experience and
training except that they were universal; and we must maintain either
that he had specialized in every occupation—as butcher's boy, wool
dealer, glove maker, horseman, dog fancier, doctor, lawyer, sailor,
musician, schoolmaster, soldier, and statesman—or that he was of so
universal a genius that he knew all things without specializing in any.

Such contentions as these might have been successfully maintained
half a century ago, but I hope to show that the most important of them
are no longer tenable and that from the plays and poems it is possible,
by the exercise of care and judgment, to learn much more about Shakespeare himself than we have been accustomed to suppose. We cannot
expect to-day to establish permanent habitations at either the north
or the south pole of his personality; but we can, I hope, make a brief
flight across the most interesting regions and fix some landmarks that
may reward us for our present efforts and perhaps guide us in future
journeys.

With this hope in view, I shall ask you to make with me a rapid
survey of the following features as displayed in the works:

1. The native endowments of the author.

2. His accomplishments and interests.

3. The changes of interest in the plays, considered in order of composition.

4. The changes of creative power in the later plays.

I shall then ask you to consider briefly how far it is possible to adjust

the personality and career revealed by the plays with the life history of William Shakespeare as vaguely given in the records and traditions.

Of the native endowments of the author of the plays the most outstanding is perhaps his exuberant vitality. This is visible not only in the enormous number of living characters created by him, but most strikingly in the effervescent, limitless vitality of single characters from every period of his work. There are Biron, Longaville, and Dumaine in *Love's Labour's Lost*, each one, singly, enough to exhaust the wit, the humor, the animal spirits of any author, and yet each only a part of a play which is itself a complete bubble of vigorous and extravagant youth. There is Mercutio, such an embodiment of fantastic, ebullient wit and humor that one critic has declared that if he had not died early in the play he could not have failed to be the death of the author. There is Sir John Falstaff, gross as a mountain, inexhaustible—"The brain of this foolish-compounded clay, man, is not able to invent anything that tends to laughter more than I invent or is invented on me: I am not only witty in myself but the cause that wit is in other men." There are Rosalind and Touchstone, Portia and Nerissa and Gratiano; and, in one of the latest plays, Perdita, a vivid incarnation of the light and color and sweetness of early spring, "Flora, peering in April's front," and Autolycus, "littered under Mercury, a snapper-up of unconsidered trifles," "once," as he says, "a servant of the prince," "then a process-server, a bailiff; then he compassed a motion of the Prodigal Son and married a tinker's wife; and having flown over many knavish professions, he settled only in rogue."

No less indicative of the author's exuberant vitality are the reckless volubility of almost every character, the piling up of fancy upon fancy, of jest upon jest, the long embellishment of humor and foolery and horseplay for no other reason than the delight they afford. "Come, come," says Mercutio to Benvolio, "thou art as hot a Jack in thy mood as any in Italy. . . . Nay, an there were two such, we should have none shortly, for one would kill the other. Thou! why, thou wilt quarrel with a man that hath a hair more or a hair less in his beard than thou hast." This would suffice any fancy of ordinary luxuriance, but to Shakespeare's teeming brain it is only a beginning:

> Thou wilt quarrel with a man for cracking nuts, having no other reason but because thou hast hazel eyes. What eye but such an eye could spy out such a quarrel? Thy head is as full of quarrels as an egg

is full of meat, and yet thy head hath been beaten as addle as an egg
for quarreling. Thou hast quarreled with a man for coughing in the
street, because he hath wakened thy dog that hath lain asleep in the
sun. Didst thou not fall out with a tailor for wearing his new
doublet before Easter? With another for tying his new shoes with
old ribands? And yet thou wilt tutor me from quarreling.

What has Queen Mab to do with the action of the play of *Romeo and
Juliet*? Nothing; but Mercutio mentions her, and before anyone can
stop him he has poured forth fifty lines of purest fantasy:

> She is the fairies' midwife, and she comes
> In shape no bigger than an agate stone
> On the forefinger of an alderman—,

and so he goes on with her horses, her chariot, her charioteer, and the
dreams she brings as she gallops night by night through lovers' brains,
o'er courtiers' knees, ladies' lips, lawyers' fingers, the parson's nose, and
the soldier's neck. "Peace, peace, Mercutio,"—interrupts Romeo—
"peace! Thou talk'st of nothing."

Whole scenes exist for no other reason than that the author's brain
is teeming with situations and characters and humor or infinite jest.
"But, Ned, to drive away the time till Falstaff come, I prithee do thou
stand in some by-room while I question my puny drawer [waiter] to
what end he gave me the sugar; and do thou never leave calling
'Francis,' that his tale to me may be nothing but 'Anon' [Coming!]."
Then follows that famous scene of purest foolery. To drive away the
time, indeed! Say rather to permit the author, that reckless spendthrift,
here as elsewhere to throw away his dramatic material with both hands,
as a drunken sailor scatters his money. No other writer in the whole
range of literature, with the possible exception of François Rabelais, is
so extravagant, so prodigal, so scornful of literary economy, or makes
upon his audience such an impression of inexhaustible vitality.

Natures of such abounding vigor are rarely distinguished by delicacy
of perception, of feeling, or of utterance. And Shakespeare often has
the coarseness of both thought and expression commonly associated
with big, rough men—horse-breeders, country-squires and the like—but
also, as everyone remembers, his plays contain a thousand delicacies of
perception, of sentiment, and of expression,—notable among which
and familiar to all are the lines spoken by Othello, as he approaches his
dreadful self-imposed task of killing Desdemona:

It is the cause, it is the cause, my soul;
Let me not name it to you, you chaste stars!
It is the cause. Yet I'll not shed her blood,
Nor scar that whiter skin of hers than snow,
And smooth as monumental alabaster,
Yet she must die, else she'll betray more men.
Put out the light, and then put out the light;
If I quench thee, thou flaming minister,
I can again thy former light restore,
Should I repent me; but once put out thy light,
Thou cunning'st pattern of excelling nature,
I know not where is that Promethean heat
That can thy light relume. When I have plucked the rose,
I cannot give it vital growth again,
It needs must wither: I'll smell it on the tree. [*Kisses her.*]
O balmy breath, that does almost persuade
Justice to break her sword! One more, one more,
Be thus when thou art dead, and I will kill thee,
And love thee after. One more, and this the last.

Closely related to this delicacy of feeling is the tenderness which appears in many phases and which is often so undramatic that it must be attributed not to the speaking character but to the author himself. You will recall many passages of sympathy with birds and other animals—the classic one being that in *As You Like It*, in which not only the melancholy Jaques but even the Duke and the nameless First Lord speak of the sufferings of the stricken deer in language which must have seemed strongly sentimental to an age devoted to hunting. That this was Shakespeare's native feeling is indicated by the long passage in *Venus and Adonis* describing the hare-hunt from the point of view of the hare—a passage recalling in its spirit the later lines addressed by Robert Burns to a field mouse.

The sympathetic understanding displayed in such passages is doubtless the result of dramatic realization working on physical senses unusually keen and powers of observation unusually fine. Keenness of sight, hearing, and smell are illustrated on every page of the plays. Examples of keenness of sight are so numerous that one hardly knows where to begin or end; but one may take at random the passage in *The Tempest* in which Caliban enumerates the riches of the island—the

springs, the berries, the crabs, the jay's nest, the nimble marmosets, the clustering filberts—or the description of the applauding crowds in *Coriolanus*, or the spreading of the news of Arthur's death in *King John*:—

> Young Arthur's death is common in their mouths;
> And when they talk of him, they shake their heads
> And whisper one another in the ear;
> And he that speaks doth gripe the hearer's wrist,
> Whilst he that hears makes fearful action
> With wrinkled brows, with nods, with rolling eyes.
> I saw a smith stand with his hammer thus,
> The whilst his iron did on the anvil cool,
> With open mouth swallowing a tailor's news;
> Who with his shears and measure in his hand,
> Standing on slippers—which his nimble haste
> Had falsely thrust upon contrary feet—
> Told of a many thousand warlike French,
> That were embattailed and rank'd in Kent.
> Another lean, unwashed artificer
> Cuts off his tale and talks of Arthur's death.

Sensitiveness of vision and images of form and color drawn from objects of all sorts we have come to expect of all poets, and most poets have been well endowed with such riches. Sensitiveness to sound is also common, but besides Shakespeare I can recall no one but Wordsworth to whose imagination sound made so constant an appeal. Every sound of the audible universe—loud and low, sweet and harsh—seems to have sprung to his thought in a multitude of associations—the big church-bell that swings of its own weight after the ringers have ceased to pull it, the carmen whistling popular tunes on the London streets, the screeching of the metal as the workman turned a brazen candlestick, a dry wheel grating on its axletree.

It is curious to note how large a part odors, pleasant and unpleasant, play in his work. He seems to have been as sensitive to them as to sounds; and indeed, as is well known, the two seem to have had similar psychological effects upon him. "That strain again," says the Duke in *Twelfth-Night,*

> That strain again! it had a dying fall:
> Oh, it came o'er my ear like the sweet sound

> That breathes upon a bank of violets,
> Stealing and giving odor.

With this should be recalled the first hundred lines of Act V, Scene 1 of *The Merchant of Venice*—wonderfully interwoven of moonlight and music and perfume and young love.

Shakespeare's susceptibility to sweet odors is shown most surprisingly in a passage in *Macbeth*. Wishing to give an idea of the fine situation and impressive architecture of Macbeth's castle, he does so by means of a conversation between Duncan and Banquo which appeals primarily to the sense of smell:

> DUN. This castle hath a pleasant seat; the air
> Nimbly and sweetly recommends itself
> Unto our gentle senses.
> BAN.   This guest of summer,
> The temple-haunting martlet does approve
> By his lov'd mansionry that the heaven's breath
> Smells wooingly here: no jutty, frieze,
> Buttress, nor coign of vantage, but this bird
> Hath made his pendent bed and procreant cradle.
> Where they most breed and haunt, I have observ'd
> The air is delicate.

In like manner, wishing to express the utmost limit of boredom, Hotspur uses a figure compounded of unpleasant sounds and unpleasant odors. He says of Glendower and his incessant talk:

> Oh, he is as tedious
> As a tired horse, a railing wife;
> Worse than a smoky house: I had rather live
> With cheese and garlic in a windmill, far,
> Than feed on cates and have him talk to me
> In any summerhouse in Christendom.

Whether Shakespeare approved of democratic ideas or not, we may at least infer that what he found most offensive about the lower classes was the filth and unpleasant odors. Coriolanus says:

> Bid them wash their faces
> And keep their teeth clean;

and again, addressing the mob of citizens:

> You common cry of curs! whose breath I hate
> As reek o' the rotten fens, whose loves I prize
> As the dead carcasses of unburied men
> That do corrupt my air;

and again in the same play Menenius expresses his deepest contempt for them in such phrases as "the breath of garlic eaters";

> You are they
> That made the air unwholesome when you cast
> Your stinking greasy caps in hooting at
> Coriolanus' exile.

This fastidiousness is not confined to Shakespeare's maturer years. Notable examples of it may be found in so early a play as *The Two Gentlemen of Verona*. Had it been a conventional fastidiousness, due merely to training and association with men of refinement, he would probably have been content, as most Elizabethans were, to have the stenches which assailed the nose at every turn overpowered by perfumes, but the description of the perfumed lord whom Hotspur met after the heat of the battle of Holmedon, and Touchstone's comments on civet may instruct us that Shakespeare's taste was for odors that were clean as well as sweet.

Of impressions of taste and touch almost no use is made in the plays. Only a very few passages could be cited showing any keenness of these senses or any vivid associations with them. This might not seem strange in lyric poetry—though even there one recalls in other poets not a few figures from touch and taste, as in Ben Jonson's *The Triumph of Charis*:

> Have you seen but a bright lily grow,
> Before rude hands have touched it?
> Have you marked but the fall of the snow,
> Before the soil hath smutch'd it?
> Have you felt the wool of the beaver?
> Or swan's down ever?
> Or have smelt o' the bud of the briar?
> Or the nard in the fire?
> Or have tasted the bag of the bee?
> Oh so white! oh so soft! oh so sweet is she!

If a man is to become a great creative artist, it is not enough that his

senses and powers of observation should be keen and extensive. He must remember, and remember vividly. Wordsworth, to be sure, speaks of poetry as taking its origin from emotion recollected in tranquillity; but in the same paragraph he not only calls it the spontaneous overflow of powerful emotions but also tells how, as the recollected emotion is contemplated, the tranquillity disappears and an emotion akin to the original one is born in the poet's mind. No one will be disposed to doubt either the vividness of Shakespeare's emotions or the tenacity of that memory which seems to have held everything, from a stray epithet in classical mythology to the look of the sham Hercules in some worm-eaten tapestry that once met his eye. For my part, I am ready to believe that he had every kind of memory known to the modern psychologist—visual, auditory, muscular—for I am confident that he did not store up in neat verbal formulas, ready for some future use, his wealth of observations of man's nature, a method practiced by Tennyson and many other writers. He rather recalled, by a process of association, when he was composing his speeches, vivid images of the objects which he was writing about, with all their color, their sharpness of outline, and their characteristic actions. This process, which I call visualization, could be illustrated from every page of his work. Indeed in any description of men or things one of the most striking features is that Shakespeare seems to describe what is present at the very moment of writing. Many of the passages already quoted would illustrate this admirably, but we may take a brief scene drawn no doubt from a memory of his youth in Gloucestershire:

> FALS. Will you tell me, Master Shallow, how to choose a man? Care I for the limb, the thews, the stature, bulk, and big assemblance of a man? Give me the spirit, Master Shallow. . . . Put me a caliver into Wart's hand, Bardolph.

This is done, and Wart obviously shows no notion of how to use it, for Shallow cries:

> He is not his craft's master, he doth not do it right. I remember at Mile-end Green, when I lay at Clement's Inn, ... there was a little quiver fellow, and a' would about and about, and come you in and come you in; 'rah tah tah' would a' say, 'bounce' would a' say, and away again would a' go, and again would a' come; I shall ne'er see such a fellow!

John M. Manly's *Shakespeare Himself*

Before leaving the matter of Shakespeare's native endowments—which might well occupy us all day—we shall note only one more feature, but that one of uncommon significance for his art. He possessed in singular combination freedom and breadth of emotional swing together with an unequalled capacity for self-criticism, for ridiculing the very emotions to which he had just given free and full indulgence. *Love's Labour's Lost* is all compact of this. Every emotion, every fancy, every fad, is entertained with zest and enthusiasm, and each in turn is heaped with ridicule or censure. *Romeo and Juliet* is the epitome of passionate and tragic love, but the play itself contains jests and mockings of the very soul of love.

That Shakespeare was not unfamiliar with tavern scenes and caroused in many a merry party at the Mermaid may be inferred not merely from tradition and from his creation of Sir John Falstaff and the world in which he moved, but above all perhaps from Sir John's famous apostrophe to the virtues of sherry wine:

> A good sherris-sack hath a two-fold operation in it. It ascends me into the brain; dries me there all the foolish, dull, and crudy vapors which environ it: makes it apprehensive, quick, forgetive, full of nimble, fiery and delectable shapes: which delivered over to the voice, the tongue, which is the birth, becomes excellent wit,—

and so on through a dozen nimble and delectable shapes which, we shall all agree, were never conceived in the brain of a teetotaler. Yet despite this evidence of his own susceptibility, it is Shakespeare who of set purpose creates the episode in *Othello* in which Cassio is disgraced by drunkenness; and it is he who puts into the mouth of this same Cassio his own condemnation:

> Drunk! and speak parrot! and squabble, swagger, swear, and discourse fustian with one's own shadow! O thou invisible spirit of wine! if thou hast no name to be known by, let us call thee devil!

And it is Shakespeare who, in play after play, with no dramatic reason or excuse, criticizes his fellow countrymen for that heavy-headed revel which makes them traduced and taxed of other nations. The traditions of Shakespeare's later life and of his death hardly allow us to take such expressions as the utterances of a reformed drunkard. We may more easily credit him with being—like the rest of us, though in a higher degree and with more vivid sensations—one who feels the attractions of

the sensual temptations of life, the cakes and the ale, but is none the less responsive to the ideal, the ethical, even the ascetic.

If we now attempt to discover from the plays the main interests and concerns of their author, we shall, I think, find them not unlike what might be expected of a man with the native qualities which we have just surveyed so sketchily and inadequately.

And first, we may state positively that the interests which above all other are exploited in the poems and in the plays down to a rather late period are those of the sportsman: horses, dogs, hunting, hawking, and, in a less degree, fishing, bowling, tennis, fencing, and archery. Most of these—especially those that predominate—were in the Elizabethan age the occupations of gentlemen, as distinguished from the common people. Bowling and tennis were more or less open to men of all ranks of society, as taverns had public bowling greens and tennis courts; archery was familiar to high and low, but had long been urged upon the middle and lower classes for reasons of state. Angling was not yet a fine art; it was merely fishing, and was within the scope of anyone who could find an unprotected stream and provide a hook and line—or, failing them, knew simpler methods of taking fish. In the light of Shakespeare's preference for other sports, his slight interest in this is not surprising. He knew it, as he knew bear-baiting, dice, and card play, but if we may judge from the evidence of the plays, he cared little about any of these things.

With horses, dogs, hunting, and hawking, the case is very different. The language of the stables, the kennel, and the hunting field runs through all the works from *Venus and Adonis* to *Othello*. It is used with a freedom and frequency unintelligible except from a sportsman; and occurs under all conceivable circumstances and in the mouths of all classes and conditions of men and women. Some of the terms and expressions are purely general, such as might be picked up by any casual member of polite society; others are so technical that they would be expected only from a professional or a skilled amateur.

The language of the stable is all pervasive. A technical interest in the qualities of horses, their breeding, their training, and their management is displayed from first to last. Of course there were then in existence books on horses, as there were books on dogs, on hunting, on hawking, and on all the other concerns of a gentleman; but no man ever became saturated with horse-talk, as Shakespeare was, by reading

a book on the horse. In the plays we find the language of the stable appropriately enough in the mouths of such persons as Petruchio, Biondello, Grumio, Falstaff, Nym, Hotspur and the Carriers; but what are we to say of its use by Touchstone, Hamlet, Rosalind, Maria, Dogberry, or the Fool in *King Lear?* For technical language let us hear Biondello, as he describes the fantastic array in which Petruchio came to fetch his bride:

> Why, Petruchio is coming, in a new hat and an old jerkin; a pair of old breeches that have been thrice turned; . . his horse hipped with an old mothy saddle and stirrups of no kindred; besides, possessed with the glanders and like to mose in the chine; troubled with the lampass, infected with the fashions, full of windgalls, sped with spavins, rayed with the yellows, past cure of the fives, stark spoiled with the staggers, begnawn with bots, swayed in the back, and shoulder-shotten; near-legged before; and with a half-checked bit, and a headstall of sheep's leather, which, being restrained to keep him from stumbling, hath been often burst and now repaired with knots: one girth six times pieced, and a woman's crupper of velure, which hath two letters of her name fairly set down in studs, and here and there pieced with pack-thread.

This is not copied from a horse-book: it is the copious extravagance of a man who had lived with horses for years.

The author's fondness for dogs and knowledge of their kinds, their habits, and their qualities are strikingly displayed in *Venus and Adonis,* and in no less than seventeen plays; and there are casual undramatic allusions to dogs in about ten other plays. In the early work the interest is that of a sportsman in the qualities of hounds; in the late, merely what may be called a recognition of dogs as members of the social organization. Compare Theseus' summary of the points of his hounds with Lear's querulous complaint of the ingratitude of his pets and Edgar's railing at dogs of all breeds. On the one hand, we have:

> THE. My hounds are bred out of the Spartan kind,
> So flew'd, so sanded, and their heads are hung
> With ears that sweep away the morning dew;
> Crook-kneed, and dew-lapp'd like Thessalian bulls;
> Slow in pursuit, but match'd in mouth like bells,
> Each under each. A cry more tuneable

Was never holla'd to, nor cheer'd with horn,
In Crete, in Sparta, nor in Thessaly.
Judge when you hear.

On the other:

            The little dogs and all,
Tray, Blanch, and Sweetheart, see, they bark at me.
EDGAR. Tom will throw his head at them.
Avaunt, you curs!
Be thy mouth or black or white,
Tooth that poisons if it bite;
Mastiff, greyhound, mongrel grim,
Hound or spaniel, brach or lym,
Or bob-tail tyke or trundle-tail;
Tom will make them weep and wail:
For, with throwing thus my head,
Dogs leap the hatch and all are fled.

Except the brief hue and cry with hunting dogs in *The Tempest*, there is, after *Lear*, not a single striking reference to dogs. The few allusions that occur are casual and often contemptuous. This is the more remarkable as the hunting scene in *Cymbeline* gives every opportunity for their effective use.

Cats are rarely mentioned and always with indifference except as to their mousing ability. The epithet "cat" is used to express extreme contempt for a man; and in *The Merchant of Venice* the phenomenon of cat fear is recognized.

Hunting terms are found in one poem and twenty-four plays. They are of the most varied character, ranging from elaborated narratives and descriptions to casual figures and images, and from technical expressions to utterances of sympathy for the hunted animals. Most of the references are to the nobler sports of hunting the deer and the hare, but there are many scattered allusions to fox-hunting—then a less systematized and less dignified branch—and even to the disreputable delights of poaching. To a vast number of the characters who use hunting terms the use of them is naturally entirely appropriate—as, for example, the courtiers and keepers of *Love's Labour's Lost*, Falstaff, the Duke in *As You Like It*, Jaques, Orlando, Rosalind, Benedick, Ford, Page, Shallow, Sir Toby, Fabyan and many others—but the appro-

priateness to Titus Andronicus, Aufidius, Scarus, Adriana, Dromio, Ulysses, Iago, Roderigo, and Prospero is not very clear. After the date of *Othello*, the references, as we shall see later, are few and slight. Specific references to hawking, the sport *par excellence* of the nobility, are fairly common and usually very technical.

All these matters have been studied in great detail and with great enthusiasm by Mr. D. H. Madden in his volume entitled *The Diary of Master William Silence*. Mr. Madden is not only convinced that the author of the plays spent a number of his youthful years in these noble sports, but is able to produce several very convincing arguments to prove that the scenes of this early training were Warwickshire and that part of Gloucestershire which lies among the Cotswold hills and which was inhabited in the sixteenth century by Justice Silence and his friends, Shallow and Slender and his humbler neighbors, William Visor of Woncot, Clement Perkes of the Hill, Goodman Double of Dursley, and Mouldy, Shadow, and Wart.

Into harmony with this view may be brought not only the general acquaintance with outdoor life and farm matters—such as might be expected of any one who in the sixteenth century had spent his boyhood in the country or in a country village—but also such specific facts as the knowledge of sheep raising, the principal industry of the Cotswold district of Gloucestershire; the assignment of the sheep-shearing of *The Winter's Tale* to a date in the summer too late for a low country like that around Stratford but entirely appropriate for the Cotswold hill region; and the rather striking though trivial circumstance of the sowing of the headland with red wheat, mentioned in *2 Henry IV*—a practice which seems to be confined, in the late summer, to this sole district of England.

Mr. Madden even argues—and to my mind convincingly—that when Queen Elizabeth commanded Shakespeare to produce in two weeks a play showing Falstaff in love, the ingenious author supplied much of the atmosphere and many of the characters of this impromptu by transferring bodily to the purlieus of Windsor the little group of Gloucestershire worthies whom Falstaff had—to our eternal advantage —so unnecessarily visited in the play that had just preceded. With this demonstration, Mr. Madden seems to have disposed for a time of the deer-stealing tradition and Shakespeare's flight from Stratford—not that the proof that Shakespeare was a poacher in his youth would put him morally lower in our estimation than the many worthy citizens

who at one time in their lives have been chased by irate owners of apple-orchards and watermelon patches, but merely because we are friendly to the truth.

If Shakespeare had been merely a sportsman, he would of course never have been the author of the plays we know. But we have already seen that he was rich in many native endowments of far different quality.

Of these the most striking are perhaps his endowments for music and art. No one can have failed to note the large extent to which music figures in the plays. Not only are about a hundred songs introduced or mentioned, not only are the whining tunes of popular ballads characterized contemptuously, not only is a general acquaintance with the terminology of music displayed, but allusions to music meet one at every turn, many long and beautiful passages are devoted to celebrating the charms and the influence of music, and characters of the most varied intelligence and training are made to exhibit such a knowledge of musical technique as could fairly be expected only of an accomplished musician. The aged John of Gaunt in *Richard II* says:

> Oh, but they say the tongues of dying men
> Enforce attention like deep harmony.

Says Mercutio of Tybalt's swordplay:

> He fights as you sing prick-song, keeps time, distance and proportion: rests me his minim rest—one, two, and the third in your bosom.

"Will you play upon this pipe?" says Hamlet to Guildenstern.
"My lord, I cannot."
"I do beseech you."
"I know no touch of it, my lord."
"'Tis as easy as lying. Govern these ventages with your finger and thumb, give it breath with your mouth, and it will discourse most eloquent music. Look you, these are the stops."
"But these cannot I command to any utterance of harmony. . . ."
"Why look you now, how unworthy a thing you make of *me*. You would play upon me; you would know my stops; you would pluck out the heart of my mystery; you would sound me from my lowest note to the top of my compass; and there is much music, excellent voice, in this little pipe, yet cannot you make it speak."

The most specific references are to singing and to instruments used for accompanying the voice. It is true that these are the times in which the development of music had reached its highest point in Elizabethan England, but the form of some of the references makes it practically certain that Shakespeare himself sang—or thought he sang—and knew enough of some instrument, the lute perhaps, to play accompaniments:

> For government, though high and low and lower,
> Put into parts, doth keep in one consent,
> Congreeing in a full and natural close,
> Like music.

> I did but tell her she mistook her frets,
> And bowed her hand to teach her fingering.

The passage which perhaps shows most vividly the author's technical familiarity with singing is in the repartee between Julia and Lucetta in *Two Gentlemen of Verona*. I quote it, italicizing the technical terms:

JUL. Some love of yours hath writ to you in rime.

LUC. That I might *sing it*, madam, *to a tune*:
Give me a note: your ladyship can *set*.

JUL. As little by such toys as may be possible;
Best *sing it to the tune of 'Light o' Love.'*

LUC. It is *too heavy for so light a tune*.

JUL. Heavy! belike it hath some *burden*, then?

LUC. Ay; and melodious were it, would you sing it.

JUL. And why not you?

LUC.   *I cannot reach so high*.

JUL. Let's see your song [*taking the letter*]. How now, minion!

LUC. *Keep time there still*, so you will *sing it out*:
And yet methinks, I do not like *this tune*.

JUL. You do not?

LUC.   No madam; it is *too sharp*.

JUL. You, minion, are too saucy.

LUC.   Nay, now you are *too flat*
And *mar the concord with too harsh a descant*:
There wanteth but *a mean to fill your song*.

JUL. *The mean is drown'd with your unruly bass*.

It may even be suspected that the elaborateness of Hortensio's tech-

nique in *The Taming of the Shrew*—if indeed it is Shakespeare's—is due to the newness of his technical knowledge of music and his consequent pride in it.

But so much is known of this matter, and the celebrated passages on music are so familiar, that we need not dwell upon it further, except to note that, like sport, music was especially affected by the upper classes.

The interest in art and the technical knowledge of it manifested by the author of the plays have attracted less attention, probably because most of the allusions are casual or figurative. Allusions to art occur in fourteen plays, in *Venus and Adonis, Lucrece,* and one sonnet; and only once—in *The Winter's Tale*—is the use of art topics motivated by the dramatic situation. The first scene of *Timon of Athens* is largely occupied, as everyone knows, with an elaborate and rather technical discussion of the relations of painting and poetry; but the most remarkable documentation of Shakespeare's interest in painting and knowledge of it is found in *The Rape of Lucrece.* Two hundred lines—nearly one-ninth of the poem—are devoted to the detailed description of a picture of the Siege of Troy. No motive for the introduction of the picture can be given, unless it is alleged that the poet must in some way indicate the passage of time before Collatine can obey the summons; but even then the choice of a picture to engage the attention of Lucrece during this time becomes significant.

The description of this picture deserves attention in many ways. Not only is the description very detailed, but the details are not such as would impress the ordinary gazer at a picture. They may be the impressions of an absolutely naïve vision which has never before been confronted by a picture, or they may represent what is seen by the trained eye of the artist, which has recovered its naive power, its capacity to see only what is actually on the canvass, and not, as ordinary eyes do, what the painter wishes to imply and suggest.

I cannot find that any English artist ever painted such a picture, but the combination of large masses with infinite individual detail recalls the work of certain Italian painters of the fifteenth and sixteenth centuries, for example Giulio Romano, the only artist named in the plays or poems. There are, indeed, grounds for believing that the author had Giulio's work in mind; but the discussion of this problem is too important to be a side-issue in the present inquiry.

Returning to the description, note the sweep of vision and the detail:

There might you see the laboring pioneer,
Begrimed with sweat and smeared all with dust;
And from the towers of Troy there would appear
The very eyes of men, through loopholes thrust,
Gazing upon the Greeks. . . .

There pleading might you see grave Nestor stand,
As 'twere encouraging the Greeks to fight;
Making such sober action with his hand
That it beguil'd attention, charm'd the sight:
In speech it seem'd his beard, all silver white,
Wagg'd up and down, and from his lips did fly
Thin winding breath, which purl'd up to the sky.

About him were a press of eager faces,
Which seem'd to swallow up his sound advice;
All jointly listening, but with several graces,
As if some mermaid did their ears entice,
Some high, some low, the painter was so nice;
The scalps of many, almost hid behind,
To hump up higher seem'd, to mark the mind.

If this is not sufficiently in the manner of the early Renaissance painters, note the following details:

Here one man's hand lean'd on another's head,
His nose being shadow'd by his neighbor's ear;
Here one, being throng'd, bears back, all boll'n and red;
Another, smother'd, seems to pelt and swear.
For such imaginary work was there;
Conceit deceitful, so compact, so kind,
That for Achilles' image stood his spear,
Gripp'd in an unseen hand; himself, behind,
Was left unseen, save to the eye of mind:
A hand, a foot, a face, a leg, a head,
Stood for the whole, to be imagined.

Is this the description of a picture which our author had seen in some great house in England or Italy? Or is it his own device, his own

vision of what some painter might put into a picture of Troy? In either event, it betrays the closest observation of the methods of Renaissance painting in general composition and individual detail; and tedious as so much quotation may have been, it seemed necessary to bring before you this significant passage from a neglected poem.

In general, the allusions to art, though brief and scattered, suggest something more than the interest of the critic; they suggest the attitude of one who knew the feeling of the brush in the hand and the application of color. This is far from saying that Shakespeare was an artist or ever had any technical training; but it is in keeping with the fact—especially characteristic of the period of the Renaissance—that a richly endowed nature often seeks expression through all the kindred arts of music, poetry, and painting. But the whole subject of the art references should be studied by one who understands the technicalities of painting.

With the passages which indicate that the author was an actor, or at least was keenly interested in the actor's art, I will not detain you. The most important of these passages—those in *As You Like It*, in *Hamlet*, and in *Troilus and Cressida*—are familiar to everyone. Allusions of this nature begin in *King John* and continue to *Antony and Cleopatra* and *The Winter's Tale*; but, as compared with the allusions to sport, they are few in number, as if the author were a little shy of "talking shop."

Phrases and figures from two fields of human—or inhuman—thought occur in such numbers in the plays as to have suggested that the author was a specialist in each; I mean the field of law and that of medicine. Was Shakespeare a learned lawyer? With due deference to Lord Campbell, I am convinced he was not. Was he a skilled physician? With due deference to Drs. Bucknill and Orville W. Owen, I am confident that he was not. That he had some knowledge of both law and medicine cannot be denied. But it may be safely asserted that in Elizabethan England every man at some time in his life became ill and went to law. The law that Shakespeare knew is perfectly accounted for by the suits—mainly about land—in which his father and he himself were involved and by the fact that in such a town as Stratford the most exciting entertainment an ambitious boy could find was a trial at court in which distinguished lawyers contended. The medicine that he knew was either such as was practiced by his mother and his wife, or such as he might as a boy have read in the garret in the cyclopedia of family medicine in vogue in his day—say Batman's version of Bartholomaeus Anglicus.

174

That the blood "visited" the heart was no anticipation of Harvey's discovery; that "the sovereign'st thing on earth was parmaceti for an inward bruise" involved the same skill in *materia medica* as is today involved in prescribing Sloan's Liniment or St. Jacob's Oil for the same ailment.

Shakespeare was not a bookish man. I will not say that he did not derive much from books; yet his debt to them shows rather that he read comparatively few but read them with eager interest and an unfailing memory than that he read many. You may cite the list Dr. Anders gives of books that he knew, but the length of this list does not shake my opinion. You yourself—whether a bookman or not—probably read as many books a year as Anders can list for Shakespeare's whole life. If it has taken scholars many years to trace all his bookish borrowings to their sources, this also is not against my contention that Shakespeare was not a bookish man. If a honey bee should fly over a field of clover and leave his sign manual on every clover head from which he sipped his honey, it would take a diligent "research man" many years to list the sources of the honey, even if the bee had visited only a hundred clover heads. Shakespeare's classical learning and his knowledge of foreign literatures are not those of a scholar but those of a man possessed of quick intelligence, boundless curiosity, and a memory tenacious of everything that engaged his interest.

Shall we inquire whether the author of the plays was a protestant or a papist, a democrat or a conservative? Articles and books have been written on these questions, but they have little bearing on our present inquiry. It is, however, possible, I believe, to show a gradual deepening of the author's thought about life, from facile and trivial epigrams, through a period of somewhat cynical worldly wisdom, to a sense of the mystery of life; but this topic we may leave for another inquirer or another occasion.

A friend who is a connoisseur in children insists that I shall not blink the fact that Shakespeare knew very little about children and except for sentimental purposes cared less. In little girls he shows scant interest; Baby Juliet is more sympathetically treated by Brooke. All the boys introduced for dramatic purposes—the young princes and Clarence's son in *Richard III*, Moth, Prince Arthur, Macduff's son, the son of Coriolanus, Mamilius—are of much the same type, pert and older than their years. The slight sketch of the stolid William struggling with Latin grammar in *The Merry Wives of Windsor*, which has no dra-

matic purpose, is the most natural portrait of a boy in the plays, and reads like an amused reminiscence of the author's school days.

One shrewd passing remark by Beatrice shows indeed keen observation, but scarcely love, of children: "—like my lady's eldest son, evermore tattling."

The changes in the kinds of subjects most often referred to casually and most often drawn upon for metaphors, comparisons, and other figures of speech are of importance for two reasons. In the first place, the fact that there are such changes, conforming roughly to the order in which the plays were probably written, proves that the method of the dramatist was not the impersonal, objective, inhuman method it is so commonly represented as being, and that interests which predominate in the plays may safely be assumed to have predominated at the same time in the thoughts of the dramatist. He wrote about horses and hounds and hawks and music and painting, not merely because some people liked such things, but because his own thoughts were at the time full of them. In the second place, the succession of interests in the plays may inform us primarily of the succession of interests in the life of the dramatist, and secondarily may be used in connection with the life records to test whether the author of the plays can have been the actor William Shakespeare who was born at Stratford-on-Avon, and who after a notable career in London retired to Stratford to lead the life of a well-to-do citizen and to die there. In both these respects it is worthy of attention that outdoor interests continue throughout the plays, but with a change of direction and form. The interest in hunting and hawking, of which the early plays are full, almost disappears after *Othello* (1604). Horses are of interest from first to last, but the dogs of the early plays are hunting dogs, hounds, and such like, while in *Lear* (1606) and later plays the few dogs that are mentioned are either house dogs or hounds that are off duty, as it were. Archery is often mentioned in *Love's Labour's Lost*, but the allusions gradually fall off and after *Hamlet* there are perhaps only three. Fencing seems to have been confined practically to the period from *Romeo and Juliet* to *Hamlet*. Fishing, which figures comparatively little at any time, comes in with *The Merchant of Venice* and increases slightly as time goes on. Agricultural phrases and figures are used practically throughout the plays and by persons in all walks of life, but after Shakespeare began to form an estate at Stratford and especially after his purchase of one hundred

and seven acres of land in 1602—or shall we say, from and after *Troilus and Cressida?*—such matters as gardening, grafting, pruning, transplanting, plowing, appear frequently; while, curiously enough, *Coriolanus* contains a number of allusions to the work of the miller.

Of the changes in power displayed by the plays I shall say little. . . . But, for the purposes of this discussion, I must remind you that the plays actually do show changes in tone and in power which cannot be without significance in regard to the author himself. We know that the early plays were partly apprentice work in retouching and revising old plays, and partly somewhat tentative and timid but still independent experiments in lines already pursued by other men; that the time before 1600 was the time of rich productiveness—counting twenty-three plays for a period of ten years or little more; that from 1600 to 1606 was the period of the greatest and most serious plays. Only six plays were produced in these six years, but all are concerned with the most serious problems of life, all are marked by a tone which approaches and often reaches pessimism; and all possess an intensity of conception and phrasing elsewhere unexampled. The plays in question need only be named to recall their problems and their mode of treatment: *Measure for Measure, Hamlet, Troilus and Cressida, Othello, Macbeth,* and *King Lear.*

From 1606 to 1609 there comes a lapse, not merely of activity, but of power. These years give us only *Timon of Athens* and *Pericles,* both written in collaboration and both containing even in their best passages only faint or sullen gleams of the ancient magical fire.

From 1609 to 1612 or 1613 we have a sort of rekindling of energy and as a result six plays: *Antony and Cleopatra, Coriolanus, The Tempest, The Winter's Tale, Cymbeline,* and part of *Henry VIII.* All of these either repeat ancient themes or are imitations of current successes, and the only one which shows the old power of creating vital human figures is *Antony and Cleopatra.* In all the other plays the *dramatis personae* are for the most part either not new or not human. Leontes is a faded Othello, Perdita a resuscitated Rosalind; Ferdinand and Miranda are sweet but thin and bloodless abstractions of forgotten youth, and Prospero exists in our imagination and memories mainly because he buried his books deeper than ever plummet sounded and spoke those unforgettable lines about the insubstantiality of material things:

> We are such stuff
> As dreams are made on, and our little life
> Is rounded with a sleep.

I have tried thus far to set before you a few of the most striking facts of personality—not a tithe of the whole evidence—evinced in the body of work which is, as all judgments agree, the most wonderful produced as yet by any mind. Is it possible that such a brain belonged to the man of Stratford? Let us briefly compare the recorded facts and traditions of his career with the testimony that, as we have seen, is embodied in the plays and poems.

The man, William Shakespeare, came of farming stock and was born and lived as boy and youth in a country village. How could it have been otherwise with the dramatist who in speaking of fair weather friends says that "they will out of their burrows, like conies after rain"? So casual an allusion could have grown only out of an experience so familiar that it had come to be a mode of thinking.

Ben Jonson says that his friend Shakespeare was lacking in education; tradition points to the Stratford grammar school as the place where he learned "small Latin and less Greek"; the plays are not merely—for an age that reveled in classical culture—unscholastic, but reveal the practical man's contempt for bookishness.

Tradition and the known facts of Shakespeare's marriage attest a wild youth, such as the old shepherd describes in *The Winter's Tale*:

> would there were no age between sixteen and three-and-twenty, or that youth would sleep out the rest: for there is nothing in the between but getting wenches with child, wronging the ancientry, stealing, fighting [*Horns*]—Hark you now! Would any but these boiled brains of nineteen and two-and-twenty hunt this weather?

As the passage is totally unwarranted by dramatic purpose, it is strongly suggestive of personal reminiscence.

In the Gloucestershire town of Dursley, in the Cotswolds, there is a belief held from time immemorial that Shakespeare spent part of his youth there; and it is a fact that a family of Shakespeares lived in that place. You will remember that in *Richard II* and in *2 Henry IV* the dramatist went out of his way to bring in these Gloucestershire wilds and their inhabitants. For what possible reason except his own abiding interest in them?

The facts show that Shakespeare early shook off provincialism and domestic ties and worked out a successful career; and the dramatist, late in life, remembers how

> the spirit of a youth
> That means to be of note, begins betimes.

The recorded facts deal with the career of the actor-manager who expresses at length in *Hamlet* views on contemporary drama, methods of acting, and the public taste.

Both facts and tradition show that Shakespeare had the friendly patronage of the Earls of Southampton, and Essex. The plays and poems reveal decided interest in the pursuits of the gentleman, and complimentary allusions to both these noblemen are not wanting.

The records show that Shakespeare lost his son Hamnet, eleven years old, in 1596. Whether or not the grief of Constance at the loss of her son was added to *King John* after that experience, we find in *Much Ado About Nothing*, written not long after Shakespeare's own loss, the dramatist expressing with an intensity, not in keeping with a comedy, a father's grief for the supposed death of a child. Again, tradition quotes Shakespeare's father as saying that "Will was a good son"; and the play of *Hamlet*, which appeared immediately after John Shakespeare's death, emphasizes far more than the source of the plot warrants the affection of a son for a father.

The records show the acquisition of landed property and the retirement from the stage of the actor-manager; and the dramatist's later plays show increased interest in agriculture, and gardening, and sheepbreeding.

The brief records of Shakespeare's later years are of money matters and of lawsuits connected with them. The plays are few in number, show a falling-off of power, and an atmosphere of pessimism and gloom. The last tradition told of him is that he died as the result of a drinking bout.

What are we to infer from all this?

It is not impossible—so much only is it safe to say—not impossible that both records and plays point to one conclusion, the exhaustion of the exuberant vitality of early life and the consequent inroads of a hypersensitive spirit upon the weakened body, resulting in premature loss of power and illness that interfered with outdoor interests and an

active life. And in that case, the lawsuits that have so troubled idealistic critics are a mere sign of the deeper irritation that

> Hath puddled his clear spirit, and in such cases
> Men's natures wrangle with inferior things.

How this may have been, perhaps we shall never know. Yet I am held by a growing conviction that infinite patience and infinite care in sifting out the personal from the dramatic elements in the Shake-spearean plays will not only identify beyond the shadow of doubting the author of them with the Stratford player, but will tell us more than we now dream it is possible to know of the man himself.

INDEX

NOTE: *"Sh" indicates Shakespeare; "in Sh" indicates references to the subject indicated in Shakespeare's writings.*